DANIEL

DANIEL

JOHN C. WHITCOMB

MOODY PUBLISHERS
CHICAGO

AllScripture quotations, unless noted otherwise, are from the *New American Standard Bible*, © 1960, 1962, 1963, 1968, 1971, 1972, 1973, 1975, and 1977 by the Lockman Foundation, and are used by permission.

Library of Congress Cataloging in Publication Data

Whitcomb, John Clement, 1924–
  Daniel.

  Bibliography: p.
  Includes index.
  1. Bible.   O.T.   Daniel—Commentaries.   I. Ttile.
BS1555.3W45   1985   224'.507   85-11462
                ISBN: 978-0-8024-2067-1 (pbk.)

We hope you enjoy this book from Moody Publishers. Our goal is to provide high-quality, thought-provoking books and products that connect truth to your real needs and challenges. For more information on other books and products written and produced from a biblical perspective, go to www.moodypublishers.com or write to:

Moody Publishers
820 N. LaSalle Boulevard
Chicago, IL 60610

20
21 23 25 27 29 30 28 26 24 22

Printed in the United States of America

CONTENTS

To our son, Dan, and his wife, Pam
Faithful servants of the Most High God
in Christian ministry

ACKNOWLEDGMENTS

The author wishes to express special appreciation to the following individuals who have made significant contributions to the the preparation of this commentary:

David L. Turner, associate professor of New Testament, Grand Rapids Baptist Theological Seminary, who carefully interacted with the entire manuscript and suggested numerous clarifications.

Robert Ibach, Jr., librarian of Grace Schools, who checked the entire manuscript at early and final editorial stages and made some helpful suggestions.

John L. Davis, president and professor of Old Testament and Hebrew, Grace Theological Seminary, who made exegetical and technical corrections in the manuscript for Daniel 1-6.

George M. Harton, assistant professor of practical theology at Capital Bible Seminary, who read the manuscript for Daniel 10-12 and offered significant corrections.

Edwin Y. Yamauchi, professor of history, Miami University, Oxford, Ohio, who recommended a number of technical background studies for Neo-Babylonian history and the book of Daniel.

Richard W. Christianson, graduate student at Grace Theological Seminary, provided the discussion on the spiritual conversion of Nebuchadnezzar (pp. 68-69), based on a special research project.

It has been a pleasure to work with Philip Rawley, Garry Knussman, and Dana Gould, textbook editors for Moody Press, and Ella K. Lindvall, managing editor. Their encouragement and helpful counsel in the preparation of the manuscript for publication have been deeply appreciated.

Finally, I wish to express appreciation to LeAnne Christianson and Bonnie Bowley, secretaries of the faculty, Grace Theological Seminary, for assisting in the preparation of the manuscript; and especially to my dear wife, Norma, whose prayerful encouragement, under God, has made the entire project possible.

INTRODUCTION

The book of Daniel stands at the very pinnacle of Old Testament prophetic writings, undergirded by the massive foundation stones of the books of Moses, most of the prophets, and the poetic books. Only Haggai, Zechariah, and Malachi follow Daniel in the prophetic stream of Old Testament revelation.

The book of Daniel must be understood in the full light of its Old Testament and ancient Near Eastern context. Daniel and his Israelite readers were intended by God to receive comfort and blessing from reading and believing these divinely revealed words. We do know that about 167 B.C. the Maccabean patriots received spiritual encouragement from the book (1 Macc. 2:59-60). Far more significant is the fact that our Lord, in referring to the Abomination of Desolation in the book of Daniel (Dan. 8-12), said: "Let the reader understand" (Matt. 24:15; Mark 13:14). He also directly quoted Daniel 7:13 when describing His second coming: "Behold, with the clouds of heaven one like a Son of Man was coming" (Matt. 24:30; 26:64; Mark 13:26; 14:62; Luke 21:27).

But although Daniel basically understood the words God spoke to him, he could not have understood the outworking of the events he described as we can today. Peter explained (1 Pet. 1:10-12) that Old Testament prophets "made careful search and inquiry, seeking to know" the messianic truths God has progressively revealed to His people, culminating in the book of Revelation. Thus, the secrets of Daniel can be brought to light adequately only by constant reference to the prophetic statements of our Lord and of the New Testament apostles and prophets. The Holy Spirit of God is His own best interpreter, and we must never allow ourselves to forget that Daniel can be understood today only in the full light of the other sixty-five God-breathed books in the library of holy Scripture.

<h2 style="text-align:center">AUTHORSHIP AND DATE</h2>

In recent decades Old Testament scholars have polarized on the volatile subject of the book's authorship and date. The last half of this century has witnessed a swing away from compromise positions by many theological conservatives with regard to the date (and thus the authorship) of the book. In the providence of God, this has brought about a renewed appreciation of the historical credibility, the structural unity, and the magnificent message of the book of Daniel.

On the other hand, theological liberals who deny the supernatural have maintained that predictive prophecy is a moral impossibility for God. Thus, the book must be a second-century B.C. product of "pious deception." The supposed purpose of the book—namely, the encouragement of Maccabean freedom fighters against the monstrous Antiochus Epiphanes—was somehow accomplished through the deception of a pseudonymous document pretending to be written by a legendary "Daniel" of four centuries earlier.

But how can one who classifies himself as a Christian make God an accomplice in such ethically questionable practices? The answer is available, and it is astounding: "Dating Daniel in the sixth century, indeed, brings not more glory to God but less. It makes it a less impressive and helpful document. It makes it seem more alien to me in my life of faith, for God does not treat me that way." John Goldingay concludes by appealing to our Lord's statement to Thomas: "Blessed are those who have not seen and yet have believed."[1]

Three answers may suffice for the liberals' reasoning. First, the basic theological thrust of the book of Daniel is that God indeed predicts events in the distant future (e.g., 2:27-28), a theme that also finds prominence in the book of Isaiah (e.g., 8:16; 29:11; 30:8; 44:6-8). The credibility of the book would be

    1. John E. Goldingay, "The Book of Daniel: Three Issues," *Themelios* 2, no. 2 (1977):49. See also our comments on Daniel 5:31.

totally shattered if its claim to be a predictive prophecy were contradicted by its date of authorship. It should also be noted that dating the book at 167 B.C. "explains away only a small part of Daniel's great prophecies [namely, 11:2-35]. The vast predictions remain concerning the first advent of the Messiah, His death, and the scattering of the Jewish people by the Romans (Dan. 9:26), which are prophecies already fulfilled."[2]

Some have quoted the Lord Jesus Christ to the effect that faith does not depend upon miracles (John 20:29). But that is totally irrelevant to the point at issue; for if our Lord meant by this what some theological liberals apparently understand Him to mean, then He would thereby have denied the reality of all biblical miracles, including the miracle of His own bodily resurrection.

A third answer is that Jews living in the intertestamental period, especially in Palestine, would never have accepted as canonical a book "hot off the press" that claimed to be over 350 years old and that was supposedly filled with historical blunders. Jewish scholars of that period had access to numerous historical records of the Neo-Babylonian, Medo-Persian, and Hellenistic periods (e.g., the writings of Herodotus, Ctesias, Xenophon, Megasthenes, Berossus, Alexander Polyhistor, Polybius, Diodorus Siculus, and at least thirty other historians referred to by Josephus, most of whose books are now lost to us).[3] Even more important, intertestamental Jews were keenly aware of the identity and boundary lines of their own sacred canon of Scripture and thus did not hesitate to exclude from their canon such books as Tobit, Judith, and even First Maccabees.

Would Jews who were dying for their God-given faith and their God-given Scriptures have looked for encouragement to fictional characters and events in a pseudograph? The truth of the matter is that nothing but *well-known* material and material that was *believed to be infallibly true* and *inspired of*

---

2. Merrill F. Unger, *Unger's Commentary on the Old Testament*, 2 vols. (Chicago: Moody, 1981), 2:1606.
3. See listing in William Whiston, trans., *The Works of Flavius Josephus*, 4 vols. (Grand Rapids: Baker, 1974), 4:469-73.

God could have kindled their spirits in the midst of that supreme hour of national crisis. It was for this very reason that the dying Mattathias appealed to the memory of Abraham, Joseph, Phinehas, Joshua, Caleb, David, and Elijah, and then concluded with these words: "Hananiah, Azariah, and Mishael believed and were saved from the flame. Daniel because of his innocence was delivered from the mouth of the lions" (1 Macc. 2:59-60, RSV). The mention of Daniel's deliverance from the lions (Dan. 6) *after* the mention of his three friends' deliverance from the fire (Dan. 3) shows that Mattathias knew of the *book* of Daniel, not merely of oral traditions concerning a prophet named Daniel.

THE UNITY OF THE BOOK

Daniel was clearly written by one author. Daniel himself is the principal character in both the historical section (1-6) and the prophetic (7-12). In chapters 1-6, Daniel interprets visions received by others, and they are written in the third person; but in chapters 7-12 he receives visions from an angelic interpreter, and they are written in the first person. Furthermore, the book displays an evident plan: the image of chapter 2 corresponds to the beasts of chapter 7, and the predictions of 7-12 are dated during the reigns of the kings mentioned in 1-6.

It is true that two languages are used (Aramaic from 2:4 to 7:28, and Hebrew elsewhere); but they do not seem to constitute any kind of natural division for the book that would require two authors. Both the Hebrew and the Aramaic wording in Daniel is much older than that of the Maccabean era (see comments on 2:4; 8:1), and even the Greek names for two of the musical instruments in Nebuchadnezzar's exotic orchestra sound forth rather loudly their Neo-Babylonian origin (see comments on 3:5).

The large majority of critical scholars have agreed that the book is indeed the product of a single author.[4] James A. Montgomery was so impressed with the pagan atmosphere pervading the first six chapters of the book (such as the "sumptuous bar-

4. Robert Pfeiffer, *Introduction to the Old Testament* (New York: Harper, 1948), p. 761.

baric scenery") that he insisted that they were not only "not of Palestine," but were "pre-Maccabean, composed in Babylonia."[5]

Going a large step further, Raymond P. Dougherty, after a very careful analysis of the fifth chapter of Daniel in the light of Neo-Babylonian documents (see comments on 5:1), concluded that it must be dated very close to the period it described. The conclusion seems obvious. A unified book, large parts of which must be dated long before the Maccabean period, which contains detailed prophecies of that period (see comments on 11:5-20), must be a book that only God could have designed.

THE HISTORICITY OF THE BOOK

In the providence of God, significant new discoveries have been made during this century that shed light on various historical statements in the book of Daniel. Discussions of these discoveries are provided at appropriate places in the commentary: (1) the chronological systems used by Daniel and Jeremiah, at 1:1; (2) Nebuchadnezzar's siege of Jerusalem, at 1:1; (3) Daniel's three-year training period in Babylon, at 1:5; (4) Ezekiel's references to Daniel, at 1:20; (5) the Aramaic section of the book, at 2:4; (6) the three Greek musical instruments in Nebuchadnezzar's orchestra, at 3:5; (7) the furnace of fire, at 3:6; (8) Nebuchadnezzar's madness, at 4:32; (9) the historical identification of Belshazzar, at 5:1; (10) the Medo-Persian conquest of Babylon, at 5:28 and 6:28; (11) the historical identification of Darius the Mede, at 5:31; (12) the den of lions, at 6:7; and (13) the unchangeable laws of the Medes and Persians, at 6:7.

God's people may be thankful that these and other such discoveries have made it all the more impossible to take seriously the "modern" critical view, originally created by the neo-Platonic philosopher Porphyry (A.D. 232-303), that the book of Daniel was a second-century B.C. pseudograph written by an

5. James A. Montgomery, *A Critical and Exegetical Commentary on the Book of Daniel,* The International Critical Commentary (Edinburgh: T. & T. Clark, 1927), pp. 90, 96.

unknown Jew and therefore susceptible to all sorts of historical blunders. "In the name of scholarship and for the sake of truth and righteousness," exclaimed Robert Dick Wilson of Princeton Theological Seminary two generations ago, "it is time to call a halt on all those who presume to a knowledge which they do not possess, in order to cast reproach upon an ancient writer, as to whose sources of information and knowledge of the facts they must be ignorant and whose statements they cannot possibly fully understand, nor successfully contradict."[6]

Careful and extended research in the archaeology and literary history of the last half of the first millennium B.C. has thus shown the hopeless impossibility of the second-century B.C. pseudograph view. But this is not the reason for a Christian's deep assurance that he has in this book the inspired, infallible, and inerrant Word of God. Such assurance comes ultimately from faith in a God who cannot lie (Titus 1:2) and from specific statements of Christ (e.g., Matt. 5:18-19) and His apostles (e.g., 2 Pet. 1:19-21) concerning the nature of canonical writings. Many recent and careful studies are available to assist God's people in their appreciation of the enormous amount of biblical material that is relevant to this vital issue.[7]

THE CANONICAL STATUS OF THE BOOK

Was the book of Daniel accepted by the Jews as canonical? There can be no hesitation in giving an affirmative answer to this important question. The Lord Jesus Christ quoted and referred to the book of Daniel, and He quoted only canonical writings. A number of fragments of Daniel have been discovered at Qumran as well as references to words that were "*written in the book of Daniel the prophet*."[8] F. F. Bruce concludes: "This expression (cf. Matt. 24:15) should put an end to doubts

6. Robert Dick Wilson, *Studies in the Book of Daniel: A Discussion of the Historical Questions* (New York: Knickerbocker, 1917), p. 149.
7. E.g., D. A. Carson and John D. Woodbridge, eds., *Scripture and Truth* (Grand Rapids: Zondervan, 1983).
8. Listed conveniently in Joyce D. Baldwin, *Daniel: An Introduction and Commentary, Tyndale OT Commentaries* (Downers Grove, Ill.: Inter-Varsity, 1978), pp. 73-74.

about the canonical status of Daniel in the Qumran community."[9]

The Hebrew Bible we now possess lists Daniel among the "writings" instead of the "prophets." "This does not necessarily mean that the individual books in the 'Writings' are all later in date or lower in authority than the component parts of the 'Prophets'. . . . For Christians it suffices that the Hebrew canon of the Old Testament was accepted as divinely authoritative by our Lord and his apostles. . . . In many points he condemned the Jewish tradition. . . . But in point of the canonicity of Scripture he confirmed their tradition, not because it was tradition, but because he believed it to be right."[10]

Many conservative Old Testament scholars believe that Daniel was not placed among the prophets in our present Hebrew Bible because he served in a foreign court, did not prophesy directly to the people of Israel, and included much historical material in his book. But significant evidence is available that Daniel was originally counted among the prophets and was only shifted to another category of canonical books by Hebrew scribes in the fourth century A.D.[11]

First, Daniel was listed among the prophets in the Septuagint translation (hence the position in our English Bibles through the medium of the Vulgate). Second, Josephus (first century

---

9. F. F. Bruce, "The Book of Daniel and the Qumran Community," in E. Earle Ellis and Max Wilcox, eds., *Neotestamentica et Semitica: Studies in Honour of Matthew Black* (Edinburgh: T. & T. Clark, 1969), p. 235 (cited in Baldwin, *Daniel*, p. 72). This highly significant introductory formula employed by the Qumran community (referring to Daniel 11:32 and 12:10) has been published in J. M. Allegro and A. A. Anderson, *Discoveries in the Judean Desert*, vol. 5: Qumran Cave 4 (Oxford: At the Clarendon Press, 1968), p. 54. F. F. Bruce's agreement that Daniel was recognized as canonical at Qumran is not, however, accompanied by a clear position on the early date of the book: "F. F. Bruce, *Israel and the Nations*, while not specifically dating Daniel, seems to indicate that the writing was after the events; see pp. 124, 133, 141, note 1" (William Sanford LaSor, et al, eds., *Old Testament Survey* [Grand Rapids: Eerdmans, 1982], p. 666).
10. F. F. Bruce, *The Books and the Parchments*, rev. and updated (Old Tappan, N.J.: Revell, 1984), pp. 94-95.
11. See, for example, the tract *Baba Bathra* 15a in the Babylonian Talmud.

A.D.) listed Daniel among the prophets. Third, Melito, bishop of Sardis (A.D. 170), did the same. Fourth, Origen (d. A.D. 254) listed Daniel before Ezekiel and the twelve prophets.[12] R. Laird Harris thus argues not only for the full canonicity of the book of Daniel but also its inclusion among the prophetic books in the most ancient Hebrew collections.[13]

In conclusion, Daniel was a canonical book of the Old Testament Scriptures as soon as it was written in the sixth century B.C., because divine inspiration guaranteed canonicity, and that is why our Lord quoted from it. The critical view that Daniel was excluded from the prophets because it was a pseudograph is a denial of all that we know of biblical theology, history, and archaeology.

The Significance of the Book

No one who has reverently studied the book of Daniel in the context of the completed Scriptures can deny the crucial contribution of this book to God's complete prophetic revelation. Our Lord spoke often of "the kingdom of heaven" (Matt. 5:3; Dan. 2:44) and of Himself as "the son of man" (Matt. 26:64; Dan. 7:13-14). Looking toward His second coming to the earth, He referred to "a great tribulation, such as has not occurred since the beginning of the world until now" (Matt. 24:21; cf. Dan. 12:1), and to "the abomination of desolation" that will stand in the Temple (Matt. 24:15; Dan. 9:27; 12:11). The apostle Paul also referred to this work of "the man of lawlessness" (2 Thess. 2:3-4; cf. Dan. 7:25; 11:36-39) but rejoiced that someday "the saints will judge the world" (1 Cor. 6:2; Dan. 7:18, 22, 27). Finally, the chronological structure and much of the symbolism of Revelation 6-19 build upon the book of Daniel (cf. Rev. 13:1-2; 17:3, 12; with Dan. 7:3-27; 9:27; 11:36-39; 12:1-7).

12. Listed and discussed in Bruce, *The Books and the Parchments,* pp. 87-95.
13. R. Laird Harris, *Inspiration and Canonicity of the Bible* (Grand Rapids: Zondervan, 1957), pp. 139-46. Harris's views are endorsed by Gleason L. Archer, *A Survey of Old Testament Introduction,* rev. ed. (Chicago: Moody, 1974), p. 380, notes 1-2.

Thirty-five years of studying and teaching biblical eschatology and the book of Daniel on a graduate level have provided ample opportunity for me to grow in my conviction that the premillennial approach to messianic prophecy is correct. To Daniel was revealed the future of Israel, not the church as such (see comments on 9:16-27). This is crucial for our appreciation of the distinctive function and destiny of the church, the spiritual Body and Bride of Christ.[14]

The similarities between Israel and the church are highly important: the same God and the same basic plan of salvation—divine election and justification by grace through the merits of Christ's blood and through faith in His Word, and regeneration and indwelling by the Holy Spirit with the hope of future glorification. But the differences are also highly important: the church is created through Christ's baptizing people in the Holy Spirit. Furthermore, the church has a new message and commission, as well as freedom from the law of Moses (including the Sabbath and other holy days, a special priesthood, and a geographically localized Holy Land and altar with animal sacrifices). God has revealed to us some of these similarities and distinctions in Romans 11 and Ephesians 2, and the book of Daniel must therefore be studied in that light.

The absolute sovereignty and transcendence of God above all angels and men literally permeates the book. For a brief moment, Nebuchadnezzar looms very large on the international horizon. He is then humbled by the God of heaven and removed. Belshazzar is weighed in God's balances and then destroyed. And so on down through the ages until "one like a Son

14. Modern critical scholarship tends to downplay the credibility of the book of Daniel because it was supposedly influenced by "the apocalyptic genre" of the late Hellenistic period. But "while Daniel abounds in apocalyptic visions, so does Zechariah 1:7—6:8 and parts of Isaiah (chaps. 24-27) and Ezekiel (chap. 37), which belong to a period long before the Greek period. The rationalistic definition of apocalyptic literature and its underlying assumptions are unacceptable to scholars who accept the book of Daniel and Zechariah 1:7—6:8 (as well as the Book of Revelation) as both authentic and truthful. . . . It must be remembered that nonbiblical apocalypses are all conscious imitations of the true Apocalypse, of which Daniel is the shining biblical model" (Merrill F. Unger, *Unger's Commentary on the Old Testament* [Chicago: Moody, 1981], 2:1605).

of Man" comes "with the clouds of heaven" and receives a kingdom "which will not pass away." What a comfort and encouragement to God's people, who struggle in the midst of the dust and clamor of a sinful world full of seemingly endless human and angelic conflicts!

OUTLINE

So powerful is the theme of divine sovereignty that the entire book can be outlined in harmony with that emphasis (note that under section II, items A, B, and C correspond to F, E, and D respectively):

Daniel: God's Rule over History [15]

I. God's Rule in Bringing Daniel to Babylon (Daniel 1)

II. God's Rule over World Empires (Daniel 2-7)

   A. Nebuchadnezzar's Dream of the Great Statue (2)
      (God's Rule over Four World Empires)

   B. Nebuchadnezzar's Golden Image (3)
      (God's Rule Preserves Daniel's Friends in the Fiery Furnace)

   C. Nebuchadnezzar's Dream of the Tree (4)
      (God's Rule Humbles Proud Nebuchadnezzar)

   D. Belshazzar's Feast (5)
      (God's Rule Judges Forgetful Belshazzar)

   E. Darius's Decree (6)
      (God's Rule Preserves Daniel in the Lions' Den)

   F. Daniel's Dream of the Four Beasts (7)

15. Outline provided by David L. Turner, associate professor of New Testament and Greek, Grace Theological Seminary, based upon Baldwin, *Daniel*, pp. 59-63, 75; and Robert D. Culver, *Daniel and the Latter Days* (Chicago: Moody, 1977), pp. 105-14. This outline has been slightly modified for use in the commentary.

III. God's Rule over Israel's Future (Daniel 8-12)

    A. Daniel's Dream of the Ram, the Male Goat, and the Little Horn (8)
       (Israel's Persecution)

    B. Daniel's Prayer and the Prophecy of the Seventy Weeks (9)
       (The End of Israel's Persecution)

    C. Daniel's Vision of the Heavenly Messenger and His Message (10-12)
       (Israel's Persecution and Restoration)

It is my prayer that this introductory study of Daniel may be used by God to encourage many of His people to master the message of this vital portion of inspired Scripture and thus to worship Him in spirit and truth, standing true to His written revelation in our day of great spiritual conflict just as Daniel did in his own day 2,500 years ago.

1

THE TRAINING OF DANIEL
IN BABYLON

I. GOD'S RULE IN BRINGING DANIEL TO BABYLON (Daniel 1)

A. DANIEL IS BROUGHT TO BABYLON (1:1-5)

1:1. In the third year of the reign of Jehoiakim. This crucial event in the history of Israel is dated by Jeremiah in the *fourth* year of Jehoiakim (Jer. 46:2; also 25:1). Many critics have looked upon this as a hopeless contradiction between the two books, thus discrediting Daniel as a dependable historical document.

Daniel, like many books in the library of Scripture, gives prominence to time relationships (relative chronology). To the student of God's Word this should bring encouragement. The Bible describes events that really happened. It is not an existential source book but rather God's inerrant record of His works in heaven and on earth. When our Lord told His disciples to "understand" the book of Daniel (Matt. 24:15), He must have included the chronological references of the book, since its chronology is the backbone of its historical (and thus theological) credibility. To study biblical chronology can thus be as "spiritual" an activity as to study its theology, for everything God put into His written Word sheds light on its total message to mankind.

Now with regard to this particular objection of the critics, it can be demonstrated that the apparent chronological discrepancy in the opening verse of the book points to two different calendar systems. Daniel used *Tishri* (October) reckoning for the beginning of Jehoiakim's official year, whereas Jeremiah used *Nisan* (April) reckoning. The reason this fact resolves the apparent discrepancy is that according to Jeremiah's Nisan reckoning, Jehoiakim's fourth official year began in the spring of 605 B.C., whereas Daniel's Tishri reckoning would place it in the fall of that year. Since all events occurring between spring and fall would automatically be one year off when these two distinct systems of chronology were used, the invasion of Nebuchadnezzar (which occurred in the summer of 605) would still be in the third year according to Daniel's system but in the fourth year according to Jeremiah's system.

But how can we be sure that these two methods of reckoning the reigns of Judean kings were actually being used at that time? According to Edwin R. Thiele, the Davidic kings of Judah started the custom of counting the fall as the appropriate time for kings to begin their reigns *officially*, namely, the first day of the seventh month (Tishri).[1] The harvest time was now ended, and the agricultural and secular life of the nation began anew. Even to this day, the Jewish New Year (Rosh Hashanah) comes in the fall, the first day of Tishri.

Proof that the Tishri system was used in Judah may be seen in the fact that a special Passover was held in the eighteenth year of Josiah (2 Kings 23:23); but several months *before* this celebration (held during Nisan, the first month of the year by Babylonian reckoning), events were already being dated in his eighteenth year (22:3). Compare also Nehemiah 1:1 with 2:1. The *religious* calendar, of course, began in the spring, the first of Nisan, in commemoration of the time of the Exodus from Egypt.

Now the kings of Assyria and Babylon used Nisan (April) instead of Tishri (October) as the appropriate time for the official commencement of the reigns of their kings. It is quite significant that Jeremiah, whose main task under God was to prepare apostate Judeans for exile to Babylon, would use the

---

1. Edwin R. Thiele, *The Mysterious Numbers of the Hebrew Kings* (Chicago: U. of Chicago, 1951). See also John C. Whitcomb, *Chart of Old Testament Kings and Prophets* and *Chart of the Babylonian Captivity* (Winona Lake, Ind.: Grace Theological Seminary, 1977, 1962).

Babylonian system (Nisan) as a warning that this foreign empire was about to take over Judea. On the other hand, Daniel would have found it appropriate to use his native Tishri system in order to encourage his fellow Jews, now in exile in Babylonia, to think in terms of the homeland to which they would eventually return (even as he faced Jerusalem thrice daily in prayer).

It is also necessary to observe that the time that elapsed between the king's accession to the throne and the first of Nisan (in Babylon) or the first of Tishri (in Judea) was called his "accession year" and did not count numerically.

Applying these principles to Jehoiakim's reign in Judah, we must note, first of all, that he did not take the throne until shortly *after* the first of Tishri, which, in the year 609 B.C., was September 21.[2] His brother Jehoahaz had been put on the throne by the Jews three months earlier, after Pharaoh Necho killed his father, Josiah, at Megiddo on a march northward to help the remnant of the Assyrian army withstand the westward push of the Babylonians (2 Chron. 35:20). At the end of the summer, Pharaoh Necho returned to Egypt.[3] On his way back through Palestine, he deposed Jehoahaz (called Shallum in Jer. 22:11) and put Jehoiakim upon the throne as a more dependable vassal (2 Kings 23:28-35).

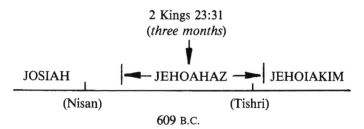

2 Kings 23:31
(*three months*)

JOSIAH |←— JEHOAHAZ —→| JEHOIAKIM

(Nisan)   (Tishri)

609 B.C.

---

2. Richard A. Parker and Waldo H. Dubberstein, *Babylonian Chronology 626 B.C.-A.D. 75* (Providence, R.I.: Brown U., 1956).

3. The Babylonian Chronicle for that year (609 B.C.) informs us that the struggle along the Euphrates continued into the month before Tishri, which was early September. See Donald J. Wiseman, *Chronicles of Chaldean Kings (626-556 B.C.)* (London: Trustees of the British Museum, 1961), p. 63.

Thus, Jehoahaz continued his reign only a few days after the beginning of his first official year on the first of Tishri (Sept. 21, 609), and Jehoiakim had to wait almost an entire year before his first official year began. That is why Jehoiakim was still in his third official year during the summer of 605 B.C. according to Daniel 1:1. But when we reckon Jehoiakim's reign according to the Nisan system, which the Babylonians (and Jeremiah) used, he had to wait less than six months to begin his first official year in the spring of 608 B.C. Thus, he would already have been in his fourth year in the summer of 605 as Jeremiah states (Jer. 46:2).

(The beginning of Jehoiakim's fourth Nisan year)	(His fourth Tishri year)
(Nisan)	(Tishri)

605 B.C.

What appears at first sign to be a serious contradiction between Jeremiah and Daniel, as negative critics have long maintained,[4] turns out rather to be a remarkable testimony to the accuracy of the Bible. Daniel, rather than Jeremiah, is the one who has usually been blamed for this so-called contradiction, because the discovery that the Tishri system was the one Judean scribes used for their kings is relatively recent.

But even if this problem had not been solved, it should be pointed out that the critical view actually proved too much. Although noting that the book of Daniel was written *after* Jeremiah, these critics did not at the same time discern that the author of Daniel (an obviously brilliant historian) would not have deliberately contradicted the chronological statements of Jeremiah unless he assumed his readers knew he was using a different system. In other words, if the book of Daniel was *not* written during the sixth century B.C., but was deliberately forged in the second century B.C. by an intelligent Jew trying to

4. See James A. Montgomery, *A Critical and Exegetical Commentary on the Book of Daniel,* The International Critical Commentary (Edinburgh: T. & T. Clark, 1927), pp. 113-16.

convince his contemporaries that his book had been written by Daniel four hundred years earlier, he would have been extremely careful to avoid obvious contradictions with the famous and canonical book of Jeremiah.

Nebuchadnezzar king of Babylon. When Nebuchadnezzar defeated the Egyptians at the Battle of Carchemish near the Euphrates River (May-June 605 B.C.), his father, Nabopolassar, was still king in Babylon. Nabopolassar died on August 15, 605, and Nebuchadnezzar hurried back to Babylon to be crowned king on September 6, 605. Technically, therefore, he was not yet "king of Babylon" when he conquered Palestine following the Battle of Carchemish. This may be explained as a *proleptic* use of the term "king" (cf. Matt. 1:6, "to Jesse was born David the king").

Came to Jerusalem and besieged it (2 Kings 24:1; 2 Chron. 36:6). It was once a commonplace of negative criticism to deny that Nebuchadnezzar could have besieged Jerusalem in 605 B.C. In 1956, however, a cuneiform tablet was published that revealed that Nebuchadnezzar "conquered the whole area of the *Hatti-country*" after the Battle of Carchemish in May-June 605. The term *Hatti-country* covers all of Syria, Phoenicia, and Palestine.[5]

1:2. And the Lord gave Jehoiakim king of Judah into his hand.

The Lord: This is the Hebrew name *Adonai;* not *Yahweh* (Jehovah), which occurs only in chapter nine. *Adonai* speaks of God as supreme master. The significance of using his name here is to say that, though outward signs did not seem to show it, God was the master of this situation, as Jehoiakim was given into the hand of Nebuchadnezzar. It was not Nebuchadnezzar's strength nor Jehoiakim's weakness that really decided the matter, but God's good pleasure. Kings like to think of themselves sufficient as rulers, but they are as much under the supreme control of God as any person. There is comfort in knowing that no governmental authority can go beyond the bounds permitted by God.[6]

5. Wiseman, *Chronicles of Chaldean Kings,* pp. 25, 68.
6. Leon Wood, *A Commentary on Daniel* (Grand Rapids: Zondervan, 1973), p. 30.

Jehoiakim, king of Judah, had been a vassal of Pharaoh Necho since the beginning of his reign in 609 B.C. Now he was taken captive by Nebuchadnezzar, who "bound him with bronze chains to take him to Babylon" (2 Chron. 36:6). It was probably because of the sudden death in Babylon of Nebuchadnezzar's father, Nabopolassar, that he was not actually deported, however. Instead, Jehoiakim was forced to swear loyalty to Nebuchadnezzar as his vassal, and Nebuchadnezzar took the short route to Babylon across the Arabian desert, sending some prisoners (including Daniel) the long way around.[7]

Jehoiakim had little intention of keeping his vows to Nebuchadnezzar, judging from the treatment he accorded the prophet Jeremiah, who counseled submission to the Babylonians. In December 604 B.C., Jehoiakim cut to pieces Jeremiah's scroll of prophecies (Jer. 36:9-32), including the prophecy of seventy years' captivity under Babylon (Jer. 25:1-11). After only three years of submission to Nebuchadnezzar, Jehoiakim attempted to throw off the yoke but was sorely chastened for his rebellion (2 Kings 24:1-2).

Along with some of the vessels of the house of God. Nebuchadnezzar shrewdly took enough of the sacred vessels to demonstrate the superiority of his god over the God of the Jews but left enough in the Temple so the Jews would be able to carry on their ceremonies unhindered and thus be less likely to rebel against their new overlord. In 586 B.C., however, totally exasperated by the disloyalty of the Jewish kings and rulers, Nebuchadnezzar ordered *all* the sacred vessels to be destroyed or carried off to Babylon (2 Chron. 36:18).

To the land of Shinar, to the house of his god. Shinar was southern Mesopotamia, or Babylonia (cf. Gen. 10:10). Here the Tower of Babel had been built (Gen. 11:2) and continued in Scripture to have "the nuance of a place hostile to faith. . . .

---

7. So according to the third-century B.C. Babylonian historian Berossus, as quoted by Josephus *Antiquities of the Jews,* X, 11, 1.

the place to which wickedness is banished" (Zech. 5:11).[8]

Nebuchadnezzar's god was *Marduk,* after whom he named his son Evil-Merodach (Amel-Marduk), because he was the chief deity of Babylon (another one was Nebo, after whom Nebuchadnezzar was named). Marduk was sometimes referred to as *Bel* (= Baal), or "Lord." Thus, Isaiah predicted the humiliating deportation of Babylonian deities in the form of idols at the time of the conquest by Cyrus in 539 B.C.: "Bel has bowed down, Nebo stoops over; their images are consigned to the beasts and the cattle. The things that you carry are burdensome, a load for the weary beast" (Isa. 46:1).

As a typical polytheist and clever diplomat, Nebuchadnezzar took no chances with Israel's God, Jehovah, and carefully enshrined His sacred vessels in Marduk's temple in Babylon. Contrast the treatment accorded these vessels sixty-six years later by Belshazzar (Dan. 5:1-4). After the fall of Babylon, King Cyrus (Ezra 1:7) and King Darius (Ezra 6:5) encouraged the Jews to carry these vessels back to their Temple in Jerusalem.

1:3. Ashpenaz, the chief of his officials. The king commanded Ashpenaz to select several handsome, brilliant, teenaged boys from the royal family to be trained as representatives of Israel in the court of Babylon (not as mere hostages). Eunuchs often held positions of great power in ancient Near Eastern kingdoms because they served as power links between the king and the harem (where most palace intrigues and plots on the king's life seemed to be hatched). Often, the term *eunuch* (the translation used in the King James Version for the Hebrew word *saris*) was applied to any important official near the king. Potiphar, for example, was a *saris* even though he was a married man (Gen. 37:36).

Because Daniel and his three friends were under the jurisdiction of "the prince of the eunuchs," and nothing is said of their having wives and children, it has been assumed by some

---

8. John F. Walvoord, *Daniel: Key to Prophetic Revelation* (Chicago: Moody, 1971), p. 32. See also Joyce G. Baldwin, *Daniel: An Introduction and Commentary, Tyndale OT Commentaries* (Downers Grove, Ill.: InterVarsity, 1978), p. 78.

scholars that they were made eunuchs by the Babylonians. This was also the opinion of Josephus, the great Jewish historian of the first century A.D. (*Antiquities* 10:10:1), and might find support in Isaiah's prophetic warning to King Hezekiah: "And some of your sons who shall issue from you, whom you shall beget, shall be taken away; and they shall become officials [eunuchs] in the palace of the king of Babylon" (Isa. 39:7).

However, the exclusion of eunuchs from positions of prominence in Israel (Deut. 23:1) and the emphasis on Daniel's physical perfection in 1:4 ("youths in whom was no defect" [Heb., *mu'mu*]) suggest that he was not a eunuch.[9] Jeremiah was not married either, and this was because God did not allow it (Jer. 16:2).

1:4. The literature and language of the Chaldeans. "These young men from Jerusalem's court needed to be secure in their knowledge of Yahweh to be able to study this literature objectively without allowing it to undermine their faith. Evidently the work of Jeremiah, Zephaniah and Habakkuk had not been in vain."[10]

The language of the Chaldeans was not Aramaic, the commercial lingua franca of the Fertile Crescent, which was somewhat similar to Hebrew and which Daniel and his friends probably knew already; it was rather the official language of Babylon, a Semitic dialect similar to Akkadian.

The term *Chaldean* is used here and in 5:30 and 9:1 (as well as in other Old Testament books and also the Assyrian records) in a national or ethnic sense. But in Daniel 2 through 5 it is used of a special class of wise men. The only other known case of this specialized use of *Chaldean* is found in a statement by the Greek historian Herodotus (b. 484 B.C.), who traveled in Babylonia and told of "the Chaldeans, the priests of this god."[11]

9. Wood, p. 33.
10. Baldwin, p. 80.
11. Herodotus *Persian Wars,* Book I, sections 181-83, trans. George Rawlinson, Francis R. B. Godolphin, ed., *The Greek Historians,* vol. 1 (New York: Random House, 1942), p. 77. See also A. R. Millard, "Daniel 1-6 and History," *The Evangelical Quarterly* 49, no. 2 (April-June 1977): 69-71.

1:5. That they should be educated three years. How could Daniel and his friends have had three years of training if they were taken to Babylon after Nebuchadnezzar became king and completed their training during the second year of his reign (compare 1:18 and 2:1)? The answer is that they were taken captive in August 605 B.C., but Nebuchadnezzar did not begin his first official year as king of Babylon until the first of Nisan in the following spring (April 4, 604). Thus, if the three years of training were academic years (inclusive reckoning), their first "year" of training could have ended just before Nisan, 604; their second year just before Nisan, 603; and their final year just before Nisan, 602, which would still have been the second official year of Nebuchadnezzar (ending April 9, 602).

B. THE DECISION OF DANIEL IN BABYLON (1:6-16)

1:7. The commander of the officials assigned new names to them.

Daniel—*(dāniyye'l)*—"God is my judge"
Belteshazzar—*(bēltᵉšaṣṣar)*—"Lady [wife of Marduk], protect the king"

Hananiah—*(hănanyāh)*—"Jehovah has been gracious"
Shadrach—*(šadrak)*—"I am very fearful (of God)"

Mishael—*(mîša'ēl)*—"Who is as God?"
Meshach—*(mēyšak)*—"I am of little account"

Azariah—*('ăzeryāh)*—"Jehovah has helped"
Abed-nego—*('ăbēd-nᵉgô)*—"Servant of the shining one (or Nabu)"[12]

In light of David's covenant that he would not take the names of other gods upon his lips (Psalm 16:4), some have assumed that Daniel and his friends would have betrayed their faith if they pronounced their own new Babylonian names. But David did not mean that he would not utter these names;

12. These etymologies are suggested by Millard, "Daniel 1-6 and History," pp. 72-73.

rather, he would not use these names in prayer, believing that they could answer and bring blessing.

The names of pagan deities are often mentioned by writers of Scripture, but always in contempt. The very fact that Daniel wrote down these new names in his own book, even though they incorporated the names of Babylonian deities (Nabu, Belet, etc.), shows that he was not superstitious in this regard. However, it is interesting to find their Hebrew names still being used twice again in this chapter and also in 2:17, whereas in 2:49 and in chapter 3 their Babylonian names are used. Daniel's Babylonian name, Belteshazzar, does not appear again until chapter 4 (vv. 8-9, 18-19) and chapter 5. But as late as the events of chapter 5 (539 B.C.), not only the queen but also King Belshazzar himself refer to him by his Hebrew name! Apparently even pagans could see that here was an Israelite whose love and loyalty to the God of his fathers could not be compromised.

> All of the Hebrew names of Daniel's companions appear again in other books of the Old Testament in reference to others of the same name. Significantly, all of their Hebrew names indicate their relationship to the God of Israel, and in the customs of the time, connote devout parents. . . . All four of the young men, however, are given new names as was customary when an individual entered a new situation. (Cf. Gen. 17:5; 41:45; 2 Sam. 12:24-25; 2 Kings 23:34; 24:17; Esther 2:7.)[13]

1:8. He would not defile himself with the king's choice food or with the wine which he drank. The point of this statement is not that Daniel was afraid of the physical effect of indulging in rich food, for he was a self-disciplined man. Nor can his refusal be based on Levitical food laws that marked some animals as ceremonially unclean, for there was no Levitical restriction against wine. Baldwin believes that "by eastern standards to share a meal was to commit oneself to friendship; it was of covenant significance. . . . The defilement he feared was not

---

13. Walvoord, p. 36. Giving someone a name was often a sign of authority. See Gen. 2:23; 3:20; 2 Kings 24:17.

so much a ritual as a moral defilement, arising from the subtle flattery of gifts and favours which entailed hidden implications of loyal support, however dubious the king's future policies might prove to be."[14] There is no biblical evidence, however, that Daniel ever insulted Nebuchadnezzar. He may have discovered that the "vegetables" (*zero'im*, grain) were not offered to idols, and trusted God to vindicate his religious convictions in abstaining from other foods.

1:9-16. Please test your servants for ten days. Though deeply sympathetic to Daniel and his friends, Ashpenaz was afraid of Nebuchadnezzar's anger if they suffered physically from the vegetarian diet. Possibly by divine direction, Daniel then asked "the overseer" (v. 11) for the special privilege of a ten-day experiment to demonstrate their physical superiority to all the other youths, who were eating the royal foods. By God's direction, this subordinate to Ashpenaz granted permission; the experiment proved successful, and the vegetable and water diet was continued for the remainder of the three-year training period.

C. THE PROGRESS OF DANIEL IN BABYLON (1:17-21)

1:17. God gave them knowledge and intelligence. Because of the special direction of God (as in the case of Joseph and Moses), Daniel and his friends found themselves immersed "in every branch of literature and wisdom" in Babylonia. C. F. Keil was correct in stating that Daniel "needed to be deeply versed in the Chaldean wisdom, as formerly Moses was in the wisdom of Egypt (Acts 7:22), so as to be able to put to shame the wisdom of this world by the hidden wisdom of God."[15]

It is unwarranted to extend the application of this unique situation to all of God's people today, however. For example, Joyce G. Baldwin believes that "the Christian today must work hard at the religions and cultures amongst which he lives, if dif-

---

14. Baldwin, p. 83 (cited by Walvoord, p. 41).
15. C. F. Keil, *Biblical Commentary on the Book of Daniel* (Grand Rapids: Eerdmans, 1955), p. 83. Cited by Walvoord, p. 41.

ferent thought worlds are ever to meet."[16] Although that may
be appropriate in certain specialized situations, the danger of
immersing one's mind in current expressions of Satan's religious perversions is enormous. It was not without reason, therefore, that God warned His people: "Beware that you . . . do
not inquire after their gods, saying, 'How do these nations
serve their gods, that I also may do likewise?' " (Deut. 12:30).
The student of comparative religions quite often, in pride and
complacency, seeks to maintain a posture of scholarly detachment and objectivity in such matters only to experience sub-
conscious and gradual spiritual poisoning. "Therefore let him
who thinks he stands take heed lest he fall" (1 Cor. 10:12).

Daniel even understood all kinds of visions and dreams. God
gave this unique privilege to Daniel, not to his friends. But even
Daniel had no automatic knowledge of all supernaturally
revealed dreams. For example, only after fervent prayer was
Nebuchadnezzar's dream revealed to him (2:17-23).

1:18-19. And the king talked with them. Though Babylon was
now the intellectual center of the world, and Nebuchadnezzar
was its most brilliant monarch, Daniel and his friends exhibited
wisdom that this great king and his kingdom had never known.
Nor was it all purely miraculous wisdom. Much hard work and
self-discipline were involved: "Do you see a man skilled in his
work? He will stand before kings" (Prov. 22:29).

1:20. He found them ten times better than all the magicians. As
in some modern European universities, it is possible that only
one examination was given—at the end of the entire program.
If a thousand questions were asked, Daniel and his friends
presumably gave nothing but correct answers (his wisdom was
God-given, according to v. 17), whereas the next highest scores
were 100 or less. On the other hand, it is quite probable that
"ten times better" is to be understood in this context as a
figure of speech, not a mathematical measurement. Compare

16. Baldwin, pp. 80-81.

3:19 where the furnace is said to have been heated seven times more than normally.[17]

About ten years after this, another Hebrew prophet in exile in Babylon, Ezekiel the priest, referred to Daniel as a righteous man comparable to Noah and Job (Ezek. 14:14, 20). Speaking sarcastically of the boasted wisdom of Ittiobalus II, king of Tyre, Ezekiel wrote: "Behold, you are wiser than Daniel; there is no secret that is a match for you" (28:3).

Many scholars have denied that these statements refer to the Daniel we know and believe they refer instead to a mythological hero in Ugaritic literature dating to the thirteenth or fourteenth centuries B.C. He is there described as "Dan 'el the Rapha-man . . . upright, sitting before the gate . . . judging the cause of the widow, adjudicating the case of the fatherless."[18]

These scholars point out that Ezekiel spells the name *Dani 'el* as in the Ugaritic myth and not *Daniyy 'el,* as in the book of Daniel. Furthermore, since Noah and Job were ancient heroes of the faith, it is claimed that it would be appropriate for the third hero mentioned by Ezekiel to be ancient also, instead of being Ezekiel's own contemporary. Liberals, of course, are predisposed to hold such a view, for they believe that the book of Daniel was not written until 164 B.C., long after the time of Ezekiel.

It is now widely conceded that even though Ezekiel's spelling is slightly different from that of his contemporary, that proves nothing; for in personal names the vowel letters were in free variation with one another, just as *Do 'eg* the Edomite (1 Sam. 21:7; 22:9) is spelled *Doyeg* in 1 Sam. 22:18, 22.[19]

---

17. For other examples of numerical hyperbole in Scripture, see Baldwin, p. 84.
18. "The Tale of Aqhat," in James B. Pritchard, *Ancient Near Eastern Texts Relating to the Old Testament,* 3d ed. (Princeton: Princeton U., 1969), pp. 149-55.
19. See "Daniel," in *The Illustrated Bible Dictionary,* 3 vols. (Wheaton: Tyndale, 1980), 1:360. "Harold H. P. Dressler ["The Identification of the Ugaritic DNIL with the Daniel of Ezekiel," *Vetus Testamentum* 29 (1979)], pp. 155-56, is right in his observations that there are no linguistic objections to the equation of the Daniel of Ezekiel 14:14, 20 and the hero of the book of Daniel. Ezekiel simply spells the name without the vowel

Even more devastating to the critical view is the recognition that the context of Ezekiel's reference to Noah, Daniel, and Job involves a powerful denunciation of the worship of Phoenician-Canaanite gods (Ezek. 14:1-13). In the light of that, Harold H. P. Dressler asks: "Is it conceivable that the same prophet would choose a Phoenician-Canaanite devotee of Baal as his outstanding example of righteousness? Within the context of Ezekiel this seems to be a preposterous suggestion."[20]

It must be recognized that Daniel's wisdom had become proverbial as early as 602 B.C. (Dan. 2:1), at least ten years before Ezekiel spoke of it (Ezek. 28:3). Thus, instead of being an embarrassment to the traditional view of the date of Daniel, Ezekiel's statement is a beautiful confirmation of it. The Scriptures themselves are their own best confirmation and authentication.

1:21. Daniel continued until the first year of Cyrus the king. In view of the fact that Daniel received his final revelation in the *third* year of Cyrus (Dan. 10:1, 536-35 B.C.), this statement is considered by some to be a contradiction within the book. The answer to this criticism is twofold:

First, even if we did not know how to solve this problem, it surely would be the better part of wisdom to assume that the

letter *yodh.* Cf. E. Lipinski, *Vetus Testamentum* 28 (1978), p. 233" (John Day, "The Daniel of Ugarit and Ezekiel and the Hero of the Book of Daniel," *Vetus Testamentum* 30 [1980], p. 181, note 18). A number of evangelical scholars have tragically wavered on this point (e.g., Horace Hummel, *The Word Becoming Flesh* [St. Louis: Concordia, 1979], pp. 271, 560; John B. Taylor, *Ezekiel: An Introduction and Commentary* [London: The Tyndale Press, 1969], p. 129; Andrew W. Blackwood, Jr., *Ezekiel: Prophecy of Hope* [Grand Rapids: Baker, 1965], pp. 102, 183; and even the footnotes on Ezek. 14:14 and 28:3 in the *New International Version* of the Bible [Grand Rapids: Zondervan Bible Publishers, 1980]; "the Hebrew spelling may suggest a person other than the prophet Daniel").

20. Harold H.P. Dressler, "The Identification of the Ugaritic DNIL with the Daniel of Ezekiel," *Vetus Testamentum* 29 (1979): 159. See also, more recently, his "Reading and Interpreting the Aqht Text: A Rejoinder to Drs. J. Day and B. Margalit," *Vetus Testamentum* 34, no. 1 (1984): 78-82.

author did not deliberately contradict himself, especially since even the negative critics agree that he was a brilliant historian.[21]

Second, there is a perfectly natural explanation for this supposed contradiction, namely, that we have here a chronological point of reference that does not demand a termination. For example, if a mother said to her child, "Now be good until I come home," she would not thereby be implying that *after* she came home the child need no longer be good. Daniel is not telling us in this verse how far into the reign of Cyrus he lived; he is simply emphasizing God's amazing providence and grace in allowing him to live throughout the entire reigns of *Nebuchadnezzar* (604-562), *Evil-merodach* (562-60), *Neriglissar* (560-56), *Labashi-marduk* (556), *Nabonidus* (556-39), *Belshazzar* (553-39)—and even beyond the termination of the Neo-Babylonian empire into the reign of *Cyrus the Great of Persia!* This is comparable only to the ministry of Joseph in the court of the pharaoh, from the age of thirty to his death at the age of one hundred and ten. Truly, then, Daniel was a man greatly honored of his God, "like a tree firmly planted by streams of water" (Ps. 1:3).

---

21. For example, Robert H. Pfeiffer, *Introduction to the Old Testament* (New York: Harper, 1948), pp. 758-59, 766.

2

NEBUCHADNEZZAR'S DREAM
OF THE GREAT IMAGE

II. God's Rule over World Empires (Daniel 2-7)

A. nebuchadnezzar's dream of the great statue (2:1-49)

1. *The Receiving of the Dream* (2:1-9)

*2:1. Now in the second year of the reign of Nebuchadnezzar
. . .* For the chronology of this momentous event, see comments on 1:5.

2:2. Then the king gave orders to call in the magicians, the conjurers, the sorcerers and the Chaldeans to tell the king his dreams.
"Magicians" (Heb., *hartummim*) was a term used of the renowned magicians (chief teaching priests) of Egypt (Gen. 41:8; Ex. 7:11). "Conjurers" (Heb., *'aššāpîm*) may refer to snake charmers. "Sorcerers" (Heb., *mekaššepîm*) could refer to ones who cut herbs for charms and spells.[1] See comments on 2:4 for "Chaldeans."

The very careful records Babylonian astronomers kept of the movements of planets, comets, and the phases of the moon were mainly for the purpose of determining the influence these "gods" might exert upon men and nations. Beginning about 747 B.C., very accurate records were handed down (and carefully recorded in Ptolemy's Almagest in the second century A.D.), so that the Babylonian astronomer Naburimannu (c. 500 B.C.)

---

1. K. A. Kitchen, "Magic and Sorcery," in *The Illustrated Bible Dictionary,* 3 vols. (Wheaton, Ill.: Tyndale, 1980), 2:931.

was able to calculate the length of the year at 365 days, 6 hours, 15 minutes, 41 seconds—only 26 minutes and 55 seconds too long!

A later Babylonian astronomer, Kidinnu (c. 390 B.C.), made some measurements even more accurate than were known in the nineteenth century A.D. "He knew the difference between the sidereal year, that is, the apparent period of revolution of the sun from the time it occupies a certain position in relation to a fixed star until it returns to that position, and the tropical year, which is the time elapsing between two successive transits of the earth through the first point of Aries. From this he discovered precession, which is the motion of the equinoxes on the ecliptic in a westward direction, that is, opposite to the sequence of the signs of the Zodiac. Furthermore, he was able to predict solar and lunar eclipses accurately."[2]

This is the caliber of men Nebuchadnezzar had in his court, which is God's way of showing us that the very best that men have to offer in the realm of worldly wisdom is utterly insufficient to solve even the most basic spiritual needs of the human heart.

2:4. Then the Chaldeans spoke to the king in Aramaic. The King James Version translates the term *Aramaic* as "Syriac" because the Greeks called the region of Aram by the name "Syria." Old Testament scholars used to call this language "Chaldee" because in this passage the Chaldeans are said to have spoken it.

It is now known that although the language of culture and scholarship in Babylon was Akkadian, Aramaic was already becoming the dominant commercial language of the empire because of its comparatively simple alphabetic script. In 701 B.C., when Sennacherib's ambassadors were confronting the people of Jerusalem, the Jewish leaders begged Rabshakeh to speak in Aramaic instead of Hebrew so that the Jews would not be able to understand their threatening words (2 Kings 18:26). At that time, therefore, very few Jews could understand Aramaic.

2. Martin Beek, *Atlas of Mesopotamia* (New York: Nelson, 1962), p. 147.

But now God was wrenching them out of their comparatively isolated corner of Palestine and exposing them to the broader cultural influences of the Fertile Crescent. One of the major new influences was the Aramaic language, which was destined to replace Hebrew as the national tongue of the Jews. By the time the remnant of Jews returned to Palestine under Zerubbabel (537 B.C.) and Ezra (458 B.C.), they needed interpreters to understand their own Hebrew Bible (Neh. 8:8). This situation continued into New Testament times, for the Lord Jesus usually spoke Aramaic.[3]

The question as to why not only the recorded words of the Chaldeans (2:4) but also the rest of the book of Daniel through chapter 7 is also in Aramaic has not been fully resolved. The best suggestion seems to be that these chapters deal more with the Gentile world in relation to Israel and therefore would have a wider interest than Daniel 1 and 8-12, which deal more strictly with Jewish affairs. This theory does not explain everything but seems to have the fewest difficulties.

For several generations, liberal critics have maintained that Aramaic words and passages in the Old Testament are a clear evidence for a third or second century B.C. date for those books. But this can no longer be accepted, for we now know that the Aramaic (as well as the Hebrew) of the book of Daniel was a much older type than that which was used during the Maccabean era (c. 165 B.C.), more closely resembling that of Ezra and the Elephantine papyri (fifth century B.C.).[4] This con-

---

3. F. F. Bruce, "The Aramaic Language," in *The Books and the Parchments,* rev. and updated (Old Tappan, N.J.: Revell, 1984), pp. 39-48.
4. The entire question has been carefully analyzed by K. A. Kitchen, "The Aramaic of Daniel," in Donald J. Wiseman et al., eds., *Notes on Some Problems in the Book of Daniel* (London: Tyndale, 1965), pp. 31-79. A. R. Millard observes that "although H. H. Rowley contested Kitchen's findings, they were supported, and Rowley's arguments refuted, by the leading Israeli Aramaist E. Y. Kutshcer in his major survey of the state of research of early Aramaic [in T. A. Seboek, ed., *Current Trends in Linguistics* 6 (The Hague, 1970), pp. 400-403] and have been favorably received by other linguists" ("Daniel 1-6 and History," *The Evangelical Quarterly* 49:2 [April-June 1977], pp. 67-68). Gleason L. Archer has contributed an important study, "The Aramaic of the 'Genesis Apocryphon' Compared with the Aramaic of Daniel," in J. Barton Payne, ed., *New Perspectives on the Old Testament* (Waco,

stitutes a shattering blow to the rationalistic presuppositions of liberal scholarship, for Daniel 2-7 contains prophecies of the rise of the Roman Empire over the Near East, which did not occur until the first century before Christ.

Among the most spectacular discoveries in the Dead Sea caves were two fragments of the book of Daniel showing the transition from Hebrew to Aramaic (2:4)[5] and then back again from Aramaic to Hebrew (8:1). As yet, the second of these fragments (along with other portions of Daniel from Cave 4) have not been published, though I had the privilege of seeing both on display at the University of Wisconsin in 1964. The archaic script of these Daniel fragments suggests a date at least as early as the first half of the second century B.C., and thus earlier than the time when the book of Daniel was supposedly forged by an unknown Jew to encourage his fellow countrymen to fight Antiochus Epiphanes.[6]

2:5. The command from me is firm. The King James Version renders this "the thing is gone from me," thus implying that

Tex.: Word, 1970), pp. 160-69, in which he demonstrates that the Aramaic of the Genesis Apocryphon (a Dead Sea scroll dating to a time shortly before Christ) is much later than the Aramaic of Daniel. Archer also points out that "the Hebrew text of Ecclesiasticus, dating from about 200-180 B.C., . . . exhibits later linguistic characteristics than Daniel, being somewhat rabbinic in tendency" (*A Survey of Old Testament Introduction*, rev. ed. [Chicago: Moody, 1974], p. 391).

5. This Dead Sea fragment showing the transition from Hebrew to Aramaic in Daniel 2:4 has been published by D. Barthelemy and J. T. Milik, *Discoveries in the Judean Desert*, vol. 1, Qumran Cave I (Oxford: Clarendon, 1955), p. 150. This fragment is called 1QDn-a (Dan. 1:10-17; 2:2-6).

6. W. S. LaSor, *Amazing Dead Sea Scrolls* (Chicago: Moody, 1956), pp. 42-44; "Daniel" in W. L. LaSor et al, eds., *Old Testament Survey* (Grand Rapids: Eerdmans, 1982), pp. 666-67; and R. K. Harrison, *Introduction to the Old Testament* (Grand Rapids: Eerdmans, 1969), p. 1118. Frank M. Cross, Jr., referring to an unpublished portion of a Daniel manuscript (4QDan,c), states: "One copy of Daniel is inscribed in the script of the late second century B.C.; in some ways its antiquity is more striking than that of the oldest manuscripts from Qumran, since it is no more than a half century younger than the autograph of Daniel." (*The Ancient Library of Qumran and Modern Biblical Studies*, rev. ed. [Grand Rapids: Baker, 1961, 1980], p. 43. One tends to wonder how much Dr. Cross may be influenced by his 167 B.C. date for the original authorship of Daniel in determining the possible date of this manuscript.

Nebuchadnezzar forgot his dream. But this seems unlikely for at least two reasons. First, we must assume that when God gives special dreams to men they will be clear, startling, and unforgettable. In fact, Daniel 2:1 informs us that the dream "troubled" him and caused him to awaken, and 2:31 tells us that what he saw was "awesome." Compare the description of Elihu (Job 33:15-18) and the experience of Pharaoh (Gen. 41).

Second, when Daniel asked Arioch about the drastic decree, "Arioch informed Daniel about the matter" (2:15), "the matter" being the same Aramaic word as "the thing" (KJV) that Nebuchadnezzar had supposedly forgotten (v. 5). It obviously refers to his decree, not his dream. The Aramaic term is *millāh* (Hebrew *dābār*) and can mean "the word" as well as "the thing" (in v. 9 *millāh* is translated "decree").

But what did Nebuchadnezzar mean when he said that "the word" (referring to the decree) "is gone from me" (KJV)? H. C. Leupold explains that "interpreters are quite commonly agreed that the rendering should be something like 'the matter has been fully determined by me.' For the difficult word '*azdā*' very likely means 'assured, certain,' being a Persian loan word. The meaning is then: 'The word is assured from me,' and that must mean, 'The thing is fully resolved upon by me.' "[7]

Thus, far from forgetting the dream, the brilliant and shrewd young king determined to use his vivid memory of it as a measuring stick against which to determine the claims of his wise men to be instruments of the gods. "It is entirely possible," John F. Walvoord observes, "that the wise men were much older than the king, having served Nebuchadnezzar's father. It would be understandable that the king might have previously been somewhat frustrated by these older counselors and may have had a real desire to be rid of them in favor of younger men whom he had chosen himself. Nebuchadnezzar might well have doubted their sincerity, honesty,

7. H. C. Leupold, *Exposition of Daniel* (Columbus: Wartburg, 1949), p. 89. For an analysis of *azda* see F. Brown, S. R. Driver, and C. A. Briggs, *A Hebrew and English Lexicon of the Old Testament* (Oxford: Clarendon, 1972), p. 1079. Joyce G. Baldwin is among those who believe that the dream was *not* forgotten by the king (*Daniel: An Introduction and Commentary*, Tyndale OT Commentaries [Downers Grove, Ill.: InterVarsity, 1978], p. 87).

and capability, and may even have questioned some of their superstitious practices. . . . It is significant that the younger wise men, such as Daniel and his companions, were not present."[8]

You will be torn from limb to limb. It was clearly understood by the wise men that Nebuchadnezzar was not speaking figuratively. More powerful than most Oriental despots and equally as cruel, Nebuchadnezzar's ability to follow through on such threats was amply confirmed by his treatment of the Judean king Zedekiah (2 Kings 25:7), Ahab and Zedekiah (two Jewish rebels in Babylon, Jer. 29:22), and the three friends of Daniel (Dan. 3).

Thus, the decree had its desired effect, and the wise men were utterly terrified and frustrated. Over a hundred years earlier, through Isaiah the prophet, God had challenged these boastful and proud men who were almost deified by the common people for their "knowledge" of heavenly affairs: "Stand fast now in your spells and in your many sorceries with which you have labored from your youth; perhaps you will be able to profit, perhaps you may cause trembling. You are wearied with your many counsels. Let now the astrologers, those who prophesy by the stars, those who predict by the new moons, stand up and save you from what will come upon you" (Isa. 47:12-13).

2:7. Let the king tell the dream . . . and we will declare the interpretation. The wise men were so experienced and clever at inventing appropriate interpretations for people's dreams that they were fully confident of their ability to escape death if the king would just tell them the nature of his dream. In fact, elaborate Akkadian manuals for interpreting various types of dreams have been discovered, thus indicating the magnitude of this ancient pseudoscience.[9] However, Nebuchadnezzar, in spite of his cleverness, was not sure that he could tell whether

8. John F. Walvoord, *Daniel: The Key to Prophetic Revelation* (Chicago: Moody, 1971), p. 50.
9. Baldwin, p. 87.

their interpretation was an invention or not; so he insisted on
hearing the dream repeated first (2:9). Such stubbornness and
ingenuity simply electrified the Chaldeans. Their final desperate appeal to reason may be paraphrased in modern par-
lance: "You are being unfair to organized magicians!" (v. 10).

It is at least possible that the Chaldeans also appealed to
Nebuchadnezzar's sympathy for and loyalty to a time-honored
profession (i.e., religious court magicians) that had served as
the very backbone of the nation in spite of the fact that they
had known all along, and the king himself deeply suspected,
that there was nothing genuinely supernatural involved in it at
all (v. 11).

But if the magicians expected this desperate appeal to the
king's sympathy and to traditional royal respect for wise men
to change his mind, they were sadly mistaken. They had at last
met their match. Nebuchadnezzar, *the head of gold* (v. 38),
was not the kind of king who would knowingly allow himself
to be manipulated by any merely human pressure group, however dignified or sanctimonious they might be. The wise men of
Babylon were doomed.

2. *The Recovery of the Dream* (2:14-23)

*2:18. In order that they might request compassion from the
God of heaven concerning this mystery.* This passage provides
for us the key to Daniel's entire career as an instrument of the
true God of Israel. He knew the supreme importance of believing prayer, preferably with other believers (v. 23, "what we re-
quested of thee"). Not until three believing men were available
to unite their prayers did mankind begin "to call upon the
name of the Lord" in a significant new way (Gen. 4:26). The
Lord Jesus told His disciples: "Where two or three have
gathered together in My name, there I am in their midst"
(Matt. 18:20; 2 Cor. 1:11).

The response of these four men to the crisis that confronted
them clearly demonstrates that, from a spiritual standpoint,
they had not been adversely affected by the three years of training in the court of Babylon. In our own day, a major cause of

apostasy in Christian schools is the subtle but intense pressure of non-Christian perspectives upon young instructors in their prolonged studies in graduate schools.

3. *The Telling of the Dream* (2:24-35)

2:24. Do not destroy the wise men of Babylon! This is one of the most remarkable statements ever uttered by Daniel. Should he not have taken advantage of this marvelous opportunity to have all of these corrupt and dangerous religious leaders removed, even as Joshua destroyed the Canaanites and Elijah killed the prophets of Baal?

The answer is that Daniel was not a prophet in the holy land of Israel, where God's infinite standards of religious truth, established at Mount Sinai, were unique among all the nations of the earth. If Daniel were to accomplish the ideal mission of a prophet of God in Israel, then all Babylonians and subject peoples throughout the empire would be forced to comply with the law of Moses or perish. But this cannot happen until the dawn of the Kingdom age, when Christ rules the world with "a rod of iron" (Isa. 11:4). Daniel was aware of this vastly important distinction and therefore (as we must also during this age of the church) allowed God to determine the times and seasons of grace and judgment. The Stone would fall in the latter days of the fourth kingdom, not the first (2:44-45).

2:28. There is a God in heaven who reveals mysteries. Daniel and his three friends were the only men in the court of Babylon who could rightfully claim access to supernatural power; but, like Joseph in the court of Pharaoh over a thousand years earlier (Gen. 41:16), he absolutely refused to take personal credit (v. 30).

This, then, must be considered the final, shattering blow to any and all pretensions of magic powers by any human being. To a limited degree, God permits Satan and his demons to imitate His works; but there never have been and never will be any "gods whose dwelling is not with flesh" (2:11) who can be manipulated by skilled magicians (cf. 1 Cor. 10:20).

2:31. You, O king, were looking and behold, there was a single great statue . . . large and of extraordinary splendor . . . and its appearance was awesome. With total confidence in the revelation of his God, Daniel briefly but accurately described the great image Nebuchadnezzar had seen, even though the wise men, conjurors, magicians, and diviners were totally frustrated in their desperate efforts to find ways to reconstruct what the king had dreamed. The size, splendor, and awesome grandeur of the image, to say nothing of God's ability to communicate effectively to men, makes it almost impossible to imagine that Nebuchadnezzar could have forgotten what he saw (see comments on 2:5).

2:32. The head of that statue was made of fine gold. Nebuchadnezzar must have been nearly overwhelmed with pride and joy to be told by Daniel: "You, O king, are the king of kings, to whom the God of heaven has given the kingdom, the power, the strength, and the glory; and wherever the sons of men dwell, or the beasts of the field, or the birds of the sky, He has given them into your hand and has caused you to rule over them all. You are the head of gold" (2:37-38).

Only six years before this, Jeremiah had warned the kings of Edom, Moab, Ammon, Tyre, and Sidon that Nebuchadnezzar had been granted sovereignty over the entire earth ("all the nations shall serve him"), and even the animal kingdom was under his dominion ("the wild animals of the field to serve him," cf. Jer. 27:6-7, 14). When Nebuchadnezzar began his siege of Jerusalem in 588 BC., God assured the Jews that even if "there were only wounded men left among them, each man in his tent, they would rise up and burn this city with fire" (Jer. 37:10). Nebuchadnezzar was divinely irresistible.

It would seem that only sinful pride, culminating in the events described in Daniel 4, prevented this great king from conquering the entire world. God wanted His people to know that it was no minor kinglet to whom He was entrusting their national chastisement.

Its breast and arms of silver. Reveling in the glorious pronouncement that he was the head of gold, Nebuchadnezzar should have been inwardly shattered to hear that his golden kingdom would come to an end. "And after you there will arise another kingdom inferior to you" (2:39). How could a real "king of kings" be replaced by anyone at all, especially by someone "inferior" to him?

The answer had already been provided by the prophet Jeremiah: "All the nations shall serve him, and his son, and his grandson, until the time of his own land comes; then many nations and great kings will make him their servant" (Jer. 27:7). After the death of Nebuchadnezzar in 562 B.C., a drastic deterioration of the qualities of the kingdom occurred under the rule of his son Evil-Merodach, two usurpers of the throne (Neriglissar and Nabonidus), and finally his daughter's son Belshazzar. By 539 B.C. the golden qualities of brilliant and absolute dictatorial autocracy which had characterized the forty-three-year reign of Nebuchadnezzar were almost gone. Then it was that "the time of his own land" finally came, and Cyrus, though inferior to Nebuchadnezzar in the authority by which he ruled (being subject to the laws of the Medes and Persians, 6:8, 15), was nevertheless overwhelmingly greater than the morally rotten Belshazzar, who was weighed in God's balances and found wanting (Dan. 5:27).

The kingdom of the Medes and Persians was thus depicted in the dream as the breast and arms of silver. The fact that the image had two arms may have been intended to indicate that the second empire would be a dual monarchy. It was also lower in monarchial quality than the early phase of the Neo-Babylonian kingdom (even as silver is about forty times less valuable than gold.[10]

Its belly and its thighs of bronze. This part of the image is explained as "another third kingdom of bronze, which will rule over all the earth" (2:39). This is the kingdom of Macedonia/Greece, which, under the leadership of Alexander the Great, beginning in 334 B.C., not only conquered the entire dual "silver" kingdom of Medo-Persia, but also regions to the

10. Allen A. Boraiko, "A Mineral of Excellent Nature: Silver," *National Geographic Magazine* 160, no. 3 (September 1981): 286.

east, as far as the borders of India. Thus, "all the earth" (from Daniel's perspective) was conquered by the "bronze" kingdom. Again, even as silver is of less value than gold, bronze (an alloy of copper and tin) is less valuable than silver. This may suggest that Alexander's kingdom would lack administrative efficiency, even though his military achievements were greater than those of his predecessors (bronze being a stronger metal for weapons than either gold or silver). For a survey of Alexander's conquests, see comments on 8:5-8.

A more complete identification and explanation of the second (silver) and third (bronze) kingdoms is provided in Daniel 8, which identifies the first of these as "the kings of Media and Persia" and the other as "the kingdom of Greece" (see comments on 8:20-21). Thus, the various visions in the book of Daniel are completely consistent in their presentation of the first three of the four kingdoms as Neo-Babylonia, Medo-Persia, and Greece/Macedonia.

2:33. Its legs of iron, its feet partly of iron and partly of clay. So significant is the fourth kingdom that the interpretation of its characteristics and functions occupy four entire verses (see comments on 2:40-43). There can be no question that this part of the image represents Rome, which endured as an identifiable government for nearly one thousand years (c. 500 B.C. to c. A.D. 500).

2:34. You continued looking until a stone was cut out without hands, and it struck the statue on its feet of iron and clay, and crushed them. Suddenly, Nebuchadnezzar's fascination with this humanlike image of decreasingly valuable metals, standing on "fragile feet of china mixed with iron," was interrupted with the vision of a great, rapidly moving stone that smashed into the feet of the image. The fact that the stone "was cut out without hands" indicates its divine character and origin, as confirmed by the explanation that it was "cut out of the mountain" (i.e., God's heavenly kingdom, Isa. 2:2) and that "the God of heaven will set up a kingdom which will never be destroyed, and . . . will itself endure forever" (2:44). The "stone" must be the "One like a Son of Man," who will receive from "the Ancient of Days . . . an everlasting dominion which will not pass away" (7:13-14). In the progress of revelation this great divine kingdom is the one our Lord taught us to pray for (Matt. 6:10) and is finally shown to have a thousand-year initial phase (the Millennium), which follows immediately the second coming of the Messiah-Christ and ultimately merges into the eternal state of the new heavens and earth (Rev. 19-22).

2:35. Then the iron, the clay, the bronze, the silver and the gold were crushed all at the same time . . . so that not a trace of them was found. It is significant that the smiting Stone crushes not only the feet and toes of iron and clay but also the entire image. This concept is repeated in the explanation in 2:45, where the reverse order from iron to gold is also repeated. This is historically, culturally, and religiously accurate. Just as the silver kingdom absorbed Neo-Babylonian religion and culture into itself (Cyrus even claimed that the gods of Babylon invited him to liberate their kingdom from Nabonidus and Belshazzar), so also Alexander the Great adapted Greek culture to Persian culture, which resulted in a new Hellenistic amalgam. And finally, Rome did not annihilate the religious, philosophic, and cultural aspects of the various Greek and Hellenistic kingdoms but incorporated them into the multifaceted empire called Rome.[11]

At the second coming of Christ, however, there will be no absorbing, adapting, modifying, merging, or restructuring of previous kingdoms. There will be total destruction. Four hundred years before Daniel, the Holy Spirit uttered these words of the coming Messiah: "I will surely tell of the decree of the Lord: He said to Me, 'Thou art my Son. . . . Ask of Me, and I will surely give the nations as Thine inheritance. . . . Thou shalt break them with a rod of iron, Thou shalt shatter them like earthenware' " (Ps. 2:7-9).

11. Edward N. Luttwak, *The Grand Strategy of the Roman Empire from the First Century A.D. to the Third* (Baltimore: Johns Hopkins U., 1976).

Thus, every trace of gold (Babylonian), silver (Medo-Persian), and bronze (Hellenistic), as well as iron and clay (Roman) influence will be removed from the earth by the Lord Jesus Christ. In that great day, all idolatry will be smashed (Isa. 2:5-22), for "the kingdom of the world" will "become the kingdom of our Lord, and of His Christ; and He will reign forever and ever" (Rev. 11:15).

But the stone that struck the statue became a great mountain and filled the whole earth. In biblical prophecy, "mountain" frequently symbolizes "kingdom" or "government" (Isa. 2:2; 27:13; Mic. 4:1). Thus, the Stone (Christ) and His government will dominate the entire earth. This is not a gradual and incomplete process (postmillennialism), but a sudden, supernatural, and all-encompassing event, so that "the earth will be full of the knowledge of the Lord as the waters cover the sea" (Isa. 11:9). The "day of man" will not evolve into the "day of the Lord" but will be suddenly and permanently replaced by it.

4. The Interpretation of the Dream (2:36-49)

2:36-39. This was the dream; now we shall tell its interpretation before the king. Daniel, by the mercy of his God, had succeeded where all the other wise men of Babylon had failed. He had given an exact description of Nebuchadnezzar's dream. Therefore the king offered no objection to Daniel's bold claim that what was about to follow was a divinely authoritative interpretation of his dream. (For comments on vv. 37-39, see above, vv. 31-32).

2:40. Then there will be a fourth kingdom as strong as iron; inasmuch as iron crushes and shatters all things, so . . . it will crush and break all these to pieces. The amazing fourth kingdom, which receives even more attention in this chapter than the future kingdom of Christ, is characterized by its ability to crush all opposition through military might. Thus, iron is stronger than gold, silver, or bronze. In a brilliant study entitled, *The Grand Strategy of the Roman Empire from the First Century A.D. to the Third,* Edward N. Luttwak explains:

The Roman army had a multitude of competent soldiers and some great generals, but its strength derived from method, not from fortuitous talent. . . . Having learned in the earlier republican period how to defeat neighbors in battle by sheer tactical strength, having later mastered the strategic complexities of large-scale warfare in fighting the Carthaginians, the Romans finally learned that the most desirable use of military power was not military at all, but political; and indeed they conquered the entire Hellenistic world with few battles and much coercive diplomacy [see comments on Dan. 11:30]. . . . It is precisely this aspect of Roman tactics (in addition to the heavy reliance on engineering warfare) that explains the relentless quality of Roman armies on the move, as well as their peculiar resiliance in adversity: the Romans won their victories slowly, but they were very hard to defeat.[12]

2:41-43. And in that you saw the feet and toes, partly of potter's clay and partly of iron, it will be a divided kingdom. . . . Some of the kingdom will be strong and part of it will be brittle . . . [the iron and the clay] will combine with one another in the seed of men; but they will not adhere to one another, even as iron does not combine with pottery. Not only does the great iron kingdom of Rome split into two legs (possibly referring to the western and eastern divisions which became fixed in A.D. 395) but ultimately into ten toes (specified in vv. 41-42). In chapter 7 the ten toes are seen in the form of ten horns. It is in the days of the ten horns that the eschatological events of Daniel 7:8, 24-27 occur, including the eleventh horn (i.e., the final Antichrist). Thus, we may conclude that the ten toes of the iron kingdom are ten future kings who will control the territory of the Roman Empire at the time of the seventieth week of Daniel (9:24-27).

The frequent mention of clay mixed with the later stages of the iron kingdom (2:33, 41-43, 45) points to political disintegration and decay. "After the death (395) of Theodosius I the empire was permanently divided into East [the Byzantine empire] and West, and Rome rapidly lost its political importance. . . . The West sank into anarchy, and Italy was ravaged

12. Ibid., pp. 2-3.

by invaders. . . . In 476 the last emperor of the West was deposed by the Goths."[13]

Nevertheless, the political disintegration of Rome was balanced by elements of strength that continue to this day and will be present to the end of this age. "It will be a divided kingdom, but it will have in it the toughness of iron" (2:41). Amazingly, then,

> The so-called Dark Ages that followed in Western Europe could not eradicate the profound imprint left by the Roman civilization. Roman law is still alive; the Romance languages are but modifications of Roman speech. Roman Catholicism for fifteen centuries was the only religion and the main cultural force of Western Europe. The fall of Rome marked no abrupt ending of an era, for the barbarians that filled the gap left by the disappearance of the old order were quick in accepting and adapting what vital elements there remained of it. The survival of the East Roman Empire and the creation of the Holy Roman Empire showed what vitality there was left in the imperial ideal.[14]

In the mysterious providence of God, the brittleness of clay (the instability of people movements?) is thus balanced by "the toughness of iron" (Roman institutions and ideals?) to maintain at least the vague identity of Rome until Christ the King of kings returns from heaven to smash and completely replace it with His perfect kingdom.

2:44-45. See comments above on 2:34-35. So overwhelming was the self-authenticating force of this divine interpretation of Nebuchadnezzar's dream that it is hardly surprising to be told, in conclusion, that "the dream is true, and its interpretation is trustworthy" (2:45). In spite of the seemingly endless attacks of modern critics, therefore, God's people may rest assured that "no [biblical] prophecy was ever made by an act of human will, but men moved by the Holy Spirit spoke from God" (2 Pet. 1:21).

13. *The Columbia Encyclopedia,* 3d ed. (New York: Columbia U., 1963), s.v. "Rome."
14. Ibid., p. 1829.

2:46. Then King Nebuchadnezzar fell on his face and did homage to Daniel. Daniel did not consider this royal homage to be idolatrous (contrast Acts 10:26), because the king immediately acknowledged that "your God is a God of gods and a Lord of kings and a revealer of mysteries" (2:47). Daniel had previously explained this vitally important fact to the king (2:28, "there is a God in heaven who reveals mysteries") and thus had prepared him for an act of true worship. (See below, on 4:37, for a discussion of the possibility of his final spiritual conversion.)

2:48. Then the king promoted Daniel . . . and he made him ruler over the whole province of Babylon and chief prefect over all the wise men of Babylon. The great crisis of 602 B.C. had now ended. The supernatural wisdom Daniel had exhibited in his academic tests (1:20) was vindicated in a spectacular fashion, and his fame spread throughout the entire Fertile Crescent. Ten years later a blasphemously proud prince of Tyre was denounced by Ezekiel with words that dripped with sarcasm: "Behold, you are wiser than Daniel; there is no secret that is a match for you" (Ezek. 28:3). Daniel's humble trust in his God opened doors of wisdom that could not be shut and brought words from heaven that will never pass away (Matt. 5:18). "Those who have insight will shine brightly like the brightness of the expanse of heaven" (Dan. 12:3). By the grace of God, even today His people have access to His wisdom in proportion to their faith in Him (James 1:5-6; 3:17).

2:49. And Daniel made request of the king, and he appointed Shadrach, Meshach and Abed-nego over the administration of the province of Babylon, while Daniel was at the king's court. Daniel's three friends had joined him in prayer for God's compassion in the hour of supreme crisis (2:17-18, 23), and now he insisted that they share with him the honor and promotion of the king. They were placed in charge of country districts, and "the separation of their spheres of work paves the way for the next chapter, in which Daniel does not feature."[15] He was not

15. Baldwin, pp. 95-96.

like the chief cupbearer in the court of Pharaoh, who forgot that Joseph had helped him in his time of need (Gen. 40:23). Infinitely more spectacular is Jesus Christ our Lord, who remembers us before the throne of God constantly (Heb. 7:25; 9:24) even though we were once His enemies (Rom. 5:10).

With Daniel firmly established as Nebuchadnezzar's chief counselor "at the king's court" and his three friends "over the administration of the province of Babylon," we can understand how no subsequent kingdom could compare with this one for quality of government. It was indeed a "head of gold."

3

DANIEL'S THREE FRIENDS
AND THE FIERY FURNACE

B. NEBUCHADNEZZAR'S GOLDEN IMAGE (3:1-30)

1. *The Erection of the Golden Image* (3:1-7)

3:1. Nebuchadnezzar the king made an image of gold. The second chapter of Daniel is dated at the beginning of Nebuchadnezzar's reign (c. 602 B.C.) and the fourth chapter at the end (568-62 B.C.). Since these two chapters deal with definite spiritual crises in the king's attitude toward the God of Israel, it would seem necessary to separate them from the *third* chapter by a sufficient amount of time for Nebuchadnezzar to forget the deep lessons he learned. An appropriate date for the events of this chapter would then be about 585 B.C., just after Jerusalem had been destroyed and the God of Israel presumably defeated and discredited.

It is entirely possible that Nebuchadnezzar, remembering the spectacular image he saw in his dream more than fifteen years earlier, attempted to duplicate it in material form. Daniel had told him that he was the head of gold (2:38) but that he would be followed by "another kingdom inferior to you" (2:39) made of silver (2:32). Rejecting now the idea that any kingdom could follow his own, he may have determined to show the permanence of his golden kingdom by having the entire image covered with gold. Thus, he clung to the more flattering aspects of the dream interpretation but dropped the rest. The fact that he was no longer honoring the God of the Jews is clear from his statement to the three friends of Daniel: "What god is there who can deliver you out of my hands?" (3:15).

The image was probably not made of solid gold but rather was *gold-plated*. If it were solid, it would have contained 5,467 cubic feet of gold (6 x 60 cubits); but all the gold mined in the past 6,000 years would bulk no larger than a cube with fifty-three-foot sides (148,877 cubic feet).[1] It is highly improbable that even the mighty Nebuchadnezzar could have managed such a display. Exodus 39:38 speaks of the "gold altar," which was actually wood overlaid with gold (Ex. 37:25-26). Idols overlaid with gold are mentioned in Isaiah 40:19 and 41:7. Jeremiah describes the same process (Jer. 10:3-9). The appearance of the image, however, was much the same as if it were solid gold.[2]

The height of which was sixty cubits and its width six cubits. The fact that the image was 6 x 60 cubits reminds us of the sexagesimal (rather than the decimal) system the Babylonians, like the Sumerians before them, used. "The number sixty was the smallest common multiple of the largest number of factors, and it was probably for this reason that the system was retained despite the many obvious advantages of the decimal system. That the sexagesimal system, once adopted, stubbornly resists displacement is very apparent from the fact that terms like dozen and gross are still very important in commercial language, not to mention the British system of weights and measures, which is still a source of trouble to foreigners. The units of time and angle handed down by the Babylonians have survived everywhere."[3]

Some critics have maintained that the story is imaginary because the proportions of the image are grotesque (ten to one), being far too narrow for a human figure. But the image may

---

1. Peter T. White, "Gold, The Eternal Treasure," *National Geographic Magazine* 145, no. 1 (January 1974): 7; and *Life Nature Series: The Earth* (New York: Time-Life, 1962), p. 96.
2. John F. Walvoord, *Daniel: The Key to Prophetic Revelation* (Chicago: Moody, 1971), p. 81. Modern technology has demonstrated that "gold can be spread exceedingly thin, so thin that light will pass through. . . . It can be processed to be . . . a film of pure gold only five millionths of an inch thick" (White, p. 2).
3. M. A. Beek, *Atlas of Mesopotamia* (New York: Nelson, 1962), p. 150.

have been set upon a pedestal, which was also of gold and thus included in the total height. Also, it is said that it was too high to be real (90 feet). But the Colossus of Rhodes (300 B.C.) was 105 feet high,[4] and Nebuchadnezzar's engineers were noted for their great skills in building towers and walls.

3:5. At the moment you hear the sound of the . . .

> horn *(qarnā')*—a trumpet, usually made of animal horn
> flute *mašrôqîtā')*—"to whistle," "to hiss"
> lyre *(qayt'rôs)*—possibly played with a plectrum (a small piece of wood or metal for plucking stringed instruments)
> trigon *(sabb'kā')*—probably a small triangular harp
> psaltery *(p'santerîn)*—another type of stringed instrument
> bagpipe *(sūm'pōnyāh)*—a percussion instrument (drum, tympanum)[5]

Since the last two of these names for instruments *(p'santerîn* and *sūm'pōnyāh)* are obviously Greek, critics have long considered this to be additional evidence that the book of Daniel could not have been written until after 332 B.C., when Alexander the Great conquered Palestine and brought Greek language and culture with him. But this view must now be abandoned in the light of many new discoveries of the close contacts Greek traders, artisans, and soldiers had with Near Eastern kingdoms several centuries *before* the time of Nebuchadnezzar.

William F. Albright, a renowned archaeologist who did not accept the inerrancy of Scripture, stated: "The idea that Greece and Hellenic culture were little known in western Asia before Alexander the Great is difficult to eradicate. . . . Greek traders and mercenaries were familiar in Egypt and throughout West-

---

4. W. H. Mare, "Rhodes," in E. M. Blaiklock and R. K. Harrison, eds., *The New International Dictionary of Biblical Archaeology* (Grand Rapids: Zondervan, 1983), p. 387.
5. See the carefully documented article by T. C. Mitchell and R. Joyce, "The Musical Instruments in Nebuchadnezzar's Orchestra," in Donald J. Wiseman et al., *Notes on Some Problems in the Book of Daniel* (London: Tyndale, 1965), pp. 19-27; and Edwin M. Yamauchi, "The Archaeological Background of Daniel," *Bibliotheca Sacra* 137, no. 545 (January-March 1980): 11-13.

ern Asia from the early seventh century on, if not earlier. As early as the sixth century B.C. the coasts of Syria and Palestine were dotted with Greek ports and trading emporia, several of which have been discovered during the past five years. . . . There were Greek mercenaries in the armies of Egypt and Babylonia, of Psammetichus II and Nebuchadnezzar."[6]

We know from Scripture that the Babylonians greatly loved beautiful and exotic music. God had said of Babylon: "Your pomp and the music of your harps have been brought down to Sheol" (Isa. 14:11); the psalmist told of the cruel Babylonian soldiers who, having heard of the great hymns sung to the God of Israel in the Temple of Jerusalem, "demanded of us songs, and our tormentors mirth, saying, 'Sing us one of the songs of Zion' " (Ps. 137:3).

In light of this, what would be more natural than for Nebuchadnezzar to gather musicians from all over the civilized world to adorn his royal orchestra in Babylon? We do know that he personally had high regard for the Greeks, for he not only had some Greek mercenaries in his army as early as 605 B.C., but also used Ionic capitals on rows of yellow columns on the decorated facade of his throne room in Babylon.[7] Thus, to say that he could not have had Greek musical instruments or even Greek musicians in his orchestra is to deny the obvious.

Perhaps the most important point to consider in this great controversy is that the book of Daniel would have been saturated with Greek terms if it were written as late as 167 B.C. in Palestine, where Greek-speaking (Hellenistic) governments had controlled the entire region for more than 160 years. Instead of this, we find just two or three technical terms referring to obviously foreign cultural objects. Thus, critical objections, deeply rooted in antisupernaturalistic presuppositions, turn out to be a providential means for displaying all the more brilliantly

6. William F. Albright, *From the Stone Age to Christianity* (New York: Doubleday, Anchor, 1957), p. 377. See also Edwin M. Yamauchi, *Greece and Babylon: Early Contacts Between the Aegean and the Near East* (Grand Rapids: Baker, 1967) and "Daniel and Contacts Between the Aegean and the Near East Before Alexander," *The Evangelical Quarterly* 53, no. 1 (January-March 1981): 37-47.

7. Yamauchi, *Greece and Babylon,* pp. 68-70.

the authenticity and genuineness of the book of Daniel as a sixth-century B.C. document.

3:6. A furnace of blazing fire. See commentary on 3:19. Also, for the significance of the change from fire to lions as a means of execution in the Medo-Persian empire, see comments on 6:7.

2. The Accusation Against the Three Friends (3:8-12)

3:12. There are certain Jews . . . Shadrach, Meshach, and Abed-nego. These men, O king, have disregarded you. It had been perhaps fifteen years or more since Nebuchadnezzar had appointed these three Jews "over the administration of the province of Babylon" (2:49). Although their service for the king was doubtless exemplary, their refusal to adopt the cultural and religious patterns of their Babylonian neighbors must have been a source of increasing animosity and bitterness, behavior their enemies could use as an excuse to destroy them. Compare the later accusation against Daniel (6:13) and still later the wild and inflammatory charge by Haman against all Jews (Esther 3:8). Behind all such anti-Jewish movements throughout history, of course, looms Satan himself, "the accuser of our brethren . . ." who accuses them before our God day and night" (Rev. 12:10). Satan knew that through this divinely chosen people would come the Messiah of Israel and the Savior of all mankind (Gen. 3:15; Rom. 9:4-5).

3. The Examination by Nebuchadnezzar (3:13-18)

3:16. O Nebuchadnezzar, we do not need to give you an answer concerning this. In the light of Jeremiah's appeal to the Jewish captives in Babylonia to submit to their rulers and even pray for them (Jer. 29:7), we may be sure that Daniel's three friends did not deliberately insult the king. The point is simply that they did not need to make a lengthy oral defense (which the king would not be capable, under such circumstances, of accepting anyway). Instead, their God would *show* the king (sooner or later) that He alone was the true God of heaven.

3:17-18. Our God whom we serve is able to deliver us from the furnace of blazing fire . . . but even if He does not. . . . At first glance, this statement sounds like a serious questioning of the omnipotence of their God (especially so in the KJV, "but if not"). But it is not the power and ability of their God but His perfect will and plan that is in question here, because these three men had *no* guarantee that God would perform a miracle on their behalf on this particular occasion, even though He obviously could have done so if He had wanted to.

In the hidden mystery of God's ways with His people (Deut. 29:29), the godly prophet Uriah was not spared the sword of Jehoiakim, even though Jeremiah was (Jer. 26:20). The apostle James was not spared the sword of Herod, even though Peter was miraculously rescued (Acts 12:2). Old Testament saints knew that miracles were rare (e.g., Judges 6:13) and could never be counted on unless God so announced. Thus, some were spared violent death at the hands of God's enemies, either miraculously or providentially, while "others were tortured, not accepting their deliverance, that they might obtain a better resurrection" (Heb. 11:35).

If we keep all of this firmly in mind, the heroism and faith of these men stands out with almost unparalleled brilliance, and a valid example is provided for all of us today. In the words of H. C. Leupold, "The quiet, modest, yet withal very positive attitude of faith that these three men display is one of the noblest examples in the Scriptures of faith fully resigned to the will of God. These men ask for no miracle; they expect none. Theirs is the faith that says: 'Though He slay me, yet will I trust in Him' (Job 13:15, KJV)."[8]

4. *The Experience of the Fiery Furnace* (3:19-30)

3:19. He answered by giving orders to heat the furnace seven times more than it was usually heated. The ancients were very skilled at regulating the temperatures of blast furnaces for smelting various metals, so it is entirely possible to interpret

8. H. C. Leupold, *Exposition of Daniel* (Columbus: Wartburg, 1949), p. 153.

this literally.[9] (But see comments on 1:20.) However, it was really an exceedingly foolish command, for the king not only lost some of his best soldiers in the process but also guaranteed that the three friends of Daniel would suffer less than they would have if the fire were subdued.

This vividly illustrates the utter inability of man to injure others beyond the limits God has set. "Do not fear those who kill the body, but are unable to kill the soul; but rather fear Him who is able to destroy both soul and body in hell" (Matt. 10:28). Indeed, "it is a terrifying thing to fall into the hands of the living God" (Heb. 10:31), because "our God is a consuming fire" (Heb. 12:29).

3:23. These three men . . . fell into the midst of the furnace of blazing fire. The superb sense of drama should not be overlooked here. Not only did they fall, but it was into the *midst* of a furnace of blazing fire. The utter helplessness of these three men could hardly be pictured more vividly. Thus, God's power to deliver is magnified, for with Him all things are possible (cf. Jer. 32:17, 27).

3:25. Look! I see four men loosed and walking about in the midst of the fire without harm. It seems probable that there was a large opening in the side of the furnace through which Nebuchadnezzar could see these men and talk to them (3:26), whereas the opening into which they had been thrown was at the top (3:23, "fell").

The experience of these men was a literal fulfillment of a beautiful promise God had made to Israel over a century earlier: "When you walk through the fire, you will not be scorched, nor will the flame burn you" (Isa. 43:2). It is doubtful that they expected God to fulfill these words literally in their case, but we may be sure that they thought about this promise from a new perspective ever afterward! Someday, the entire nation of Israel will enter into its "furnace of blazing fire" (i.e., the Great Tribulation), and God's power to bring

9. John B. Alexander, "Critical Notes: New Light on the Fiery Furnace," *Journal of Biblical Literature* 69, no. 4 (December 1950): 375-76.

His own through that time of trial will be obvious to all (Isa. 4:3-5).

This miracle of deliverance made a profound impression upon the people of Israel, for we read this statement in the second-century B.C. book of First Maccabees: "Hananiah, Azariah, and Mishael believed and were saved from the flame" (2:59). (One might observe that the remarkably accurate author of First Maccabees could hardly have used this event to encourage his compatriots to resist the vicious attacks of Antiochus Epiphanes if he suspected that the events recorded by Daniel really never occurred.) Still later, the inspired book of Hebrews speaks of some who "quenched the power of fire" (11:34), referring, doubtless, to the account in Daniel 3.

And the appearance of the fourth is like a son of the gods! In view of the fact that the preincarnate Christ had previously appeared in a burning bush (Ex. 3) and had ascended in a flame of fire (Judg. 13), there is no biblical reason He could not have been the one who appeared in the furnace with these men. However, it is also probable that Nebuchadnezzar would not have been capable of identifying God's Son even if he did see Him. In verse 28 he refers to Him as God's "angel" (i.e., "messenger"). There may have been something about His appearance that suggested a supernatural being, though this is not necessary. After all, only three men had been thrown in the furnace, so the fourth *must* have come from the unseen world.

3:27. Nor was the hair of their head singed . . . nor had the smell of fire even come upon them. When our God delivers miraculously, He delivers completely! Not one Israelite perished in the Red Sea. Not one Assyrian soldier survived to attack Jerusalem in the days of Hezekiah. Not one of the 144,000 will perish in "the Day of Jacob's Trouble." In countless cases when our Lord Jesus Christ healed the sick and raised the dead, there was complete healing. Spiritually speaking, such examples are great and reassuring to God's people.

3:28-30. There is no other god who is able to deliver in this way. Needless to say, the ceremony came to a sudden halt. Instead of worshiping the beautiful golden image, the people of Babylon were now commanded to honor the God of Israel under a threat identical to that made several years earlier to the court magicians (2:5). Life in Babylonia under a monarch like Nebuchadnezzar must have been religiously traumatic—one could not know from one day to the next which god to worship and did not dare to make a mistake! It would be interesting to know how many Babylonians truly sought to honor the God of Israel as a result of this decree by comparison with the response of the Ninevites to the preaching of Jonah.

4

NEBUCHADNEZZAR'S DREAM
OF THE HIGH TREE

C. NEBUCHADNEZZAR'S DREAM OF THE TREE (4:1-37)

1. *The Circumstances Surrounding the Dream* (4:1-9)

4:1-3. These are the last recorded words of Nebuchadnezzar, for they were written after the events described in this chapter. Because of the similarity of expression with earlier portions of the Old Testament (e.g., Ps. 145:13), it is possible that the king enlisted the help of Daniel, his faithful minister in charge of Jewish affairs, to prepare the decree in words that would be honoring to the God of Israel and understandable to all Jews.

4:4. I . . . was at ease in my house and flourishing in my palace. This must have occurred near the end of his long reign (605-562), for the great goal of his reign, the rebuilding of Babylon, was now accomplished (4:30). If his insanity continued for seven years ("seven times" suggests years in light of 7:25), and the dream was experienced twelve months before the insanity (4:29), then this year must have been 570/569 B.C. About two years before this, Nebuchadnezzar's long and only partly successful siege of Tyre had ended (Ezek. 29:17-18). God compensated him by giving him the land of Egypt (Ezek. 29:19-20) in fulfillment of Jeremiah's prophecy (Jer. 43:10; 44:29-30).

It must have been shortly after receiving this warning dream (which he describes in vv. 10-17) that Nebuchadnezzar hurried down to Egypt to suppress a revolt. A fragmentary tablet has been discovered which reads: "In the 37th year [which began April 23, 568 B.C.], Nebuchadnezzar, King of Babylon marched against Egypt to deliver a battle."[1] Upon his return to Babylon, flushed with victory and pride, he made his fateful boast: "Is this not Babylon the great, which I myself have built?" (4:30).

4:8. But finally Daniel came in before me. Even as King Ahab had refused to call the prophet Micaiah because he suspected that the message would be ominous (1 Kings 22:8), so Nebuchadnezzar waited until the very last moment to call Daniel to interpret his dream of the tree.

In whom is the spirit of the holy gods. If the king is attempting here to honor Daniel's God, the phrase could just as well be translated, "the Spirit of the holy God" (cf. 4:9, 18; 5:11, 14).

4:9. Tell me the visions of my dream which I have seen, along with its interpretation. The king had already told the magicians what his dream was, and is about to tell Daniel also. Thus, a better translation of this verse might be: "Behold the visions of my dream that I have seen, and the interpretation thereof declare."

But why does the king not repeat the test of chapter 2 and withhold the content of the dream as well? The answer may well be that his earlier test had settled once for all the difference between Daniel and the other magicians, and he now wanted these magicians to flatter him and soothe his conscience.

2. The Content of the Dream (4:10-18)

4:10. There was a tree in the midst of the earth, and its height was great. "The use of trees in the Bible for symbolic purposes," Walvoord explains, "is found frequently (cf. 2 Kings 14:9; Pss. 1:3; 37:35; 52:8; 92:12; Ezek. 17). An obvious

---

1. James B. Pritchard, ed., *Ancient Near Eastern Texts Relating to the Old Testament,* 3d ed. (Princeton: Princeton U., 1969), p. 308. See also the discussion in Donald J. Wiseman, *Chronicles of Chaldean Kings (626-566 B.C.)* (London: British Museum, 1961).

parallel to Nebuchadnezzar's dream is recorded in Ezekiel 31, where the Assyrian as well as the Egyptian Pharaoh are compared to a cedar of Lebanon."[2]

4:13. Behold, an angelic watcher, a holy one, descended from heaven. Critics have attempted to prove from this verse that polytheism underlies the text of the Old Testament. Upon closer inspection, however, we discover that "watcher" and "holy one" refer to "one person only, because all verbs employed regarding him are singular. . . . The participant to which reference is made must be an angel, but it should be noted that only in this chapter is this way of referring to an angel used. It is possible that Nebuchadnezzar, the speaker, may have been influenced in this manner of reference by concepts characteristic of the East of his day . . . however, the two qualities, watchfulness and holiness, fit well as descriptive of God's angels."[3]

In his interpretation of the dream, Daniel says it was "the decree of the Most High" that descended from heaven (v. 24), "thus bypassing the intermediaries" and emphasizing God as the sovereign ruler of all angelic agencies in exercising judgment upon men.

3. *The Interpretation of the Dream* (4:19-27)

4:26. Your kingdom will be assured to you. This is Daniel's explanation of the "band of iron and bronze" that the king had seen around "the stump with its roots in the ground" (4:23). "The interpretation of the stump with its bands of iron and brass is that Nebuchadnezzar will retain control of his kingdom and that it will be restored to him after he comes back to his senses. To have had his mind restored to him without the kingdom would have been a hollow victory. In spite of his pride, Nebuchadnezzar was to know the graciousness of God to him."[4]

2. John F. Walvoord, *Daniel: The Key to Prophetic Revelation* (Chicago: Moody, 1971), p. 101.
3. Leon J. Wood, *A Commentary on Daniel* (Grand Rapids: Zondervan, 1973), pp. 108-9.
4. Walvoord, p. 106.

4:27. Break away now from your sins by doing righteousness.
Daniel is not stating here that righteous acts on a social or
political level will bring salvation. Instead, he is warning
Nebuchadnezzar that his life would be cut short if he continued
his cruel and self-centered deeds. It is true, of course, that only
genuine conversion would bring about the desired change. For
discussion of Nebuchadnezzar's possible conversion, see 4:37.

4. *The Fulfilling of the Dream* (4:28-37)

*4:30. Is not this Babylon the great, which I myself have built as
a royal residence by the might of my power and for the glory of
my majesty?* This was not simply an idle boast. Mainly through
the systematic excavations of the German archaeologist Robert
Koldewey, from 1899 to 1917, much of the ruins of Nebuchadnezzar's Babylon have been recovered. The following features
are especially noteworthy:

1. The city was protected by a system of great double walls,
the outer line extending ten miles around. The double walls
were each 25 feet thick, with 40 feet between, and a total of
260 towers 160 feet apart.

2. Through the center of the city, for two-thirds of a mile, extended the great 70-feet-wide stone-paved Procession Street,
having walls decorated with enameled bricks showing 120 lions
and 575 dragons and bulls arranged in alternate rows. Andre
Parrot explains that "the figure of each animal stood out
against a uniform background tinted blue with powdered lapis
lazuli. The architecture and ornamentation were skillfully
adapted to each other, and the animals were carved to scale,
and despite their multitude the arrangement was orderly and
harmonious ."[5] At the northern end of the Procession Street
was the famous Ishtar Gate, 35 feet high, decorated with 557
animals in bright colors against a glazed blue background. The
original gate was brought by Koldewey to Berlin, where it still

5. Andre Parrot, *Nineveh and Babylon* (New York: Western, Golden,
1961), p. 174.

resides, but an exact replica may be seen at the Oriental Institute Museum of the University of Chicago.

3. The city was dominated by a seven-story ziggurat (step-pyramid), 288 feet high, known as the Tower of Babylon. Nearly 60 million fired bricks were used to construct this huge tower, and on top of it stood the Temple of Marduk (E-temen-an-ki, "house of the foundation of heaven and earth"), containing a solid gold statue of Marduk, which weighed 52,000 pounds (according to fifth-century B.C. Greek historian Herodotus).

4. At the north end of the city, near the Ishtar Gate, was Nebuchadnezzar's palace. His throne room was 171 by 56 feet, having "a triple gateway and a richly decorated facade of glazed bricks. Yellow columns whose superimposed Ionic capitals were crowned by palmettes were linked to each other by a garland of lotus buds."[6] "At the northeast angle of the palace are the remains of vaults thought by Koldewey to be supports for the terraced 'hanging gardens' built by Nebuchadnezzar for Amytis, his Median wife, as a reminder of her homeland."[7] It was built upon stone arches and was equipped with a draw well and chain pump. The Hanging Gardens of Babylon were counted as one of the seven wonders of the ancient world.

The accuracy of this boast by Nebuchadnezzar, recorded in the book of Daniel, has thus been brilliantly confirmed through archaeological excavation, for it was not previously known that he was personally responsible for rebuilding so much of the city.[8] Ancient historians had referred to him only

6. Ibid., p. 176.
7. Donald J. Wiseman, "Babylon," in *The Illustrated Bible Dictionary*, 3 vols. (Wheaton, Ill.: Tyndale, 1980), 1:161. On the Hanging Gardens, see the third-century B.C. Babylonian historian Berossus, as quoted by Josephus *Against Apion*, 1:19.
8. For a clear photograph of a kiln-fired brick, stamped with an inscription commemorating the rebuilding of the temples of Marduk and Nabu by Nebuchadnezzar in Babylon, see *The Illustrated Bible Dictionary*, 2:1065. Also for a photograph of one of the twelve-inch-square bricks inscribed with the name and titles of Nebuchadnezzar, see Donald J. Wiseman, *Illustrations from Biblical Archaeology* (Grand Rapids: Eerdmans, 1958), p. 71.

as a great general and conqueror. Robert H. Pfeiffer of Harvard University, a leading representative of the liberal wing of Old Testament scholarship in America a generation ago, frankly admitted: "We shall presumably never know how our author learned that the new Babylon was the creation of Nebuchadnezzar (4:30), as the excavations have proved."[9] The author of the book of Daniel knew this, of course, because he *was* Daniel, the chief of Nebuchadnezzar's wise men.

4:31. While the word was in the king's mouth. Frequently in Scripture God is said to bring judgment at the very moment blasphemous words issue from the mouths of His creatures. Compare the Israelites in the wilderness, Psalm 78:30-31; Ananias and Sapphira, Acts 5; and Herod Agrippa, Acts 12:23. The amazing thing about God's longsuffering is that such words and deeds are permitted at all.

4:32. You will be given grass to eat like cattle. The name for this rare form of insanity is *bo-anthropy* ("ox-man"), whereby the victim, inwardly normal in consciousness, behaves like an ox, eating grass as his exclusive diet.[19]

Many Old Testament scholars have been persuaded that it was Nabonidus (556-539 B.C.), not Nebuchadnezzar (605-562 B.C.), who experienced this time of insanity. This idea is based on the publication in 1956 of a document discovered at the fourth cave of Qumran known as "The Prayer of Nabonidus," in which Nabonidus is said to have been "smitten with a serious inflammation by the command of the Most High God in the city of Teima" in Arabia and that this required his segregation from men until seven "times" had passed.

But R. K. Harrison gives adequate reasons for branding this document as folklore and cites several fragments of contemporary evidence and later tradition in support of the biblical ac-

9. R. H. Pfeiffer, *Introduction to the Old Testament* (New York: Harper, 1948), pp. 758-59.
10. R. K. Harrison, *Introduction to the Old Testament* (Grand Rapids: Eerdmans, 1969), pp. 1116-17.

count of Nebuchadnezzar's madness.[11] The reader must keep
clearly in mind the fact that negative critics of the Bible are bound
to a second-century B.C. authorship of the book of Daniel, and
any fragment of information that might be used to impugn the authenticity of the book is used for that purpose.

4:36. My counselors and my nobles began seeking me out. During
these years of Nebuchadnezzar's madness, Daniel may have been
the one who actually controlled the direction of the government,
for he was the only one who knew when the king would emerge
from his insanity, after seven "times" had elapsed. It would have
been embarrassing (to put it mildly) for any government official to
neglect his responsibilities or speak against the king, if the
resumption of the king's official functions could occur at any
moment. "Do not complain . . . that you yourselves may not
be judged; behold, the Judge is standing right at the door"
(James 5:9).

*4:37. Now I Nebuchadnezzar praise, exalt, and honor the King of
heaven.* Was Nebuchadnezzar genuinely converted by the Holy
Spirit on this occasion? God's people have pondered this question
through the centuries. In the final analysis, of course, only God
knows. Some reputable and devout students of the book of Daniel
(e.g., Calvin, Hengstenberg, Pusey, and Leupold) have believed
that Nebuchadnezzar probably was not truly converted, because
he seems not to have recognized the grace and the mercy that God
had extended to him. Furthermore, if the spiritual state of a person
can be known only by the spiritual fruit he continues to manifest,
Nebuchadnezzar did not live long enough after his "conversion"
to bear much of this fruit.

On the other hand, it can be argued that Nebuchadnezzar did in
fact recognize that God had dealt with him graciously. After all,
he fully acknowledged that he was again on his throne because an
absolutely sovereign God had chosen to put him there (4:34-36),
and he admitted that this special divine favor was wholly

11. Ibid., pp. 1117-20. See also Joyce G. Baldwin, *Daniel: An Introduction
and Commentary, Tyndale OT Commentaries* (Downers Grove, Ill.: InterVarsity, 1978), pp. 116-18.

undeserved (4:35). Also, though Nebuchadnezzar did not live long after he was restored to his throne, he did bear some spiritual fruit. The verbs "praise," "exalt," and "honor" in verse 37 occur in a form that emphasizes the continuing nature of these activities.[12] Thus not only did Nebuchadnezzar worship God when he was delivered from his insanity (4:34), but also he *continued* to worship God even to the very day on which he issued his decree (4:37).

Further, Edward J. Young and John F. Walvoord, among others, believe that a progression in Nebuchadnezzar's spiritual perception can be traced toward a climax in this passage. And referring to Nebuchadnezzar, the Lord said to Daniel in a dream that this "lion" with "the wings of an eagle" was "made to stand on two feet like a man; a human mind also was given to it" (7:4). Does this not imply a complete transformation of his nature?

Thirteen years later, the aged Daniel explained to Belshazzar that Nebuchadnezzar experienced insanity "until he recognized that the Most High God is ruler over the realm of mankind. . . . Yet you, his son, Belshazzar, have not humbled your heart, even though you knew all this" (5:21-22). Is Daniel saying here that Nebuchadnezzar experienced true conversion and that Belshazzar desperately needed this too? Walvoord concludes:

> Nebuchadnezzar reaches a new spiritual perspicacity. Prior to his experience of insanity, his confessions were those of a pagan whose polytheism permitted the addition of new gods, as illustrated in Daniel 2:47 and 3:28-29. Now Nebuchadnezzar apparently worships the King of heaven only. For this reason, his autobiography is truly remarkable and reflects the fruitfulness of Daniel's influence upon him and probably of Daniel's daily prayers for him. Certainly God is no respecter of persons and can save the high and mighty in this world as well as the lowly.[13]

12. Woods, p. 124.
13. Walvoord, p. 112.

5

BELSHAZZAR'S FEAST

D. BELSHAZZAR'S FEAST (5:1-31)

1. *The Description of the Feast* (5:1-4)

5:1. Belshazzar the king. Because he was a subordinate king under his father, Nabonidus, during the final fourteen years of the Neo-Babylonian empire (553-539 B.C.), Belshazzar's name was soon forgotten by ancient Babylonian and Greek historians who were interested mainly in the reigns of *official* kings. Negative critics of the Bible considered this silence to be fatal to the claim of the book of Daniel to be a sixth-century B.C. document, since it refers to Belshazzar as "the Chaldean king" when Babylon fell (5:30) and dates events in the first and third years of his reign (7:1 and 8:1).

But as early as 1861, H. F. Talbot published a cuneiform tablet found at Ur containing the name BEL-SHAR-USUR ("Bel protect the king!"). In 1882, Theophilus Pinches published the famous "Nabonidus Chronicle" and correctly inferred that the "crown prince" (obviously Belshazzar) "was regarded as king" because he was left in full control of the army in Babylon from at least 549 to 545 B.C. while Nabonidus was establishing a new military and commercial fortress at Teima in northwest Arabia.[1]

Still more texts appeared which contained the name "Belshazzar" and shed important light on his activities as the *mar-sharri* (son of the king). In 1916, Pinches published two legal documents dated in the twelfth and thirteenth years of

---

1. *Transactions of the Society of Biblical Archaeology* (1882), 7:150.

Nabonidus (544-543 B.C.), which record oaths sworn by the life of Nabonidus, the king, and of Belshazzar, the crown prince. A. L. Oppenheim observes, "There is no known parallel for this in all ancient cuneiform literature."[2]

The final blow to critical objections to the historicity of the fifth chapter of Daniel came in 1924, when Sidney Smith of the British Museum published a cuneiform document known as the "Persian Verse Account of Nabonidus," which contains the statement that Nabonidus "entrusted the kingship" to Belshazzar. This crucially important statement reads as follows: "When the third year [553 B.C.] was about to begin, he [Nabonidus] entrusted the 'Camp' to his eldest son, the first-born, the troops everywhere in the country he ordered under his command. He let everything go, entrusted the kingship [*sarrutum*] to him and, himself, he started out for a long journey."[3]

Old Testament scholars of the more liberal school have been divided in their reaction to this spectacular evidence. Norman W. Porteous insists that the fifth chapter of Daniel is "not history but story-telling for the communication of religious truth" because "in the story before us Belshazzar is represented as acting in every way as a king with full authority," whereas the inscriptional evidence shows that "he was never king, though a certain royal dignity was accorded him."[4] Robert H. Pfeiffer of Harvard University more cautiously concluded: "We shall presumably never know how our author learned . . . that Belshazzar, mentioned only in Babylonian records, in Daniel, and in Baruch 1:11, which is based on Daniel, was functioning as king when Cyrus took Babylon."[5] But J. Finegan states much more positively: "Since, therefore, Belshazzar actually exercised the co-regency at Babylon and

2. A. L. Oppenheim, "Belshazzar," in George A. Buttrick and Keith R. Crim, eds., *The Interpreter's Dictionary of the Bible,* 5 vols. (New York: Abingdon, 1962), 1:380.
3. James B. Pritchard, ed., *Ancient Near Eastern Texts Relating to the Old Testament,* 3d ed. (Princeton: Princeton U., 1969), p. 313.
4. Norman W. Porteous, *Daniel: A Commentary* (Philadelphia: Westminster, 1965), pp. 76ff.
5. R. H. Pfeiffer, *Introduction to the Old Testament* (New York: Harper, 1948), pp. 758ff.

may well have continued to do so unto the end, the Book of Daniel (5:30) is not wrong in representing him as the last king of Babylon.''[6]

The book of Daniel represents Nebuchadnezzar as Belshazzar's "father" (5:2, 11, 18, 22), but this is not a historical blunder, as some have claimed.[7] In his definitive study of this period of history, Raymond P. Dougherty showed that Nabonidus probably married Nitocris, a daughter of Nebuchadnezzar.[8] Thus, "one need not be surprised that the fifth chapter of Daniel calls Nebuchadnezzar the father instead of the grandfather of Belshazzar, as this is entirely in harmony with Semitic usage under such circumstances."[9]

Furthermore, the omission of any reference to Nabonidus and Belshazzar's offer to make Daniel "third ruler in the kingdom" (5:7, 16, 29) shows that "the fifth chapter of Daniel is in remarkable harmony" with the known fact that "Nabonidus was the titular head of the nation, but Belshazzar, who had been delegated with royal authority by his father, was the second ruler."[10]

Many have insisted that the book of Daniel is in error when it states that "in that night Belshazzar the Chaldean king was slain" (5:30), for this supposedly contradicts the report in the Nabonidus Chronicle that Babylon fell into the hands of the Persians without a general conflict. But our text says nothing of a battle. It simply states that Belshazzar was slain. A similar situation occurred when Queen Athaliah was slain in Jerusalem (2 Kings 11:15-16). Dougherty denies that "the writer of the fifth chapter of Daniel thought that Babylon was captured as the result of vigorous combat involving the full strength of opposing armies. The bare reference to the slaying of Belshazzar is not enough to sustain such an interpretation."[11]

6. Jack Finegan, *Light from the Ancient Past,* 2d ed. (Princeton: Princeton U., 1959), p. 228.
7. Porteous, p. 77.
8. Raymond P. Dougherty, *Nabonidus and Belshazzar* (New Haven, Conn.: Yale U., 1929), pp. 42ff.
9. Ibid., p. 194.
10. Ibid., p. 196.
11. Ibid., p. 198.

Half a century of additional research on the Belshazzar problem has produced nothing to modify Raymond Dougherty's conclusion:

> Of all non-Babylonian records dealing with the situation at the close of the Neo-Babylonian empire *the fifth chapter of Daniel ranks next to cuneiform literature in accuracy* as far as outstanding events are concerned. The Scriptural account may be interpreted as excelling because it employs the name Belshazzar, because it attributes royal power to Belshazzar, and because it recognizes that a dual rulership existed in the kingdom. Babylonian cuneiform documents of the sixth century B.C. furnish clearcut evidence of the correctness of these three basic historical nuclei contained in the Biblical narrative dealing with the fall of Babylon. . . . The total information found in all available chronologically-fixed documents later than the cuneiform texts of the sixth century B.C. and prior to the writings of Josephus of the first century A.D. could not have provided the necessary material for the historical framework of the fifth chapter of Daniel. The view that the fifth chapter of Daniel originated in the Maccabean age is discredited. Biblical critics have pushed back its date to the third century B.C. . . . However, a narrative characterized by such an accurate historical perspective as Daniel 5 ought to be entitled to a place much nearer in time to the reliable documents which belong to the general epoch with which it deals.[12]

Held a great feast for a thousand of his nobles, and he was drinking wine in the presence of the thousand. In Assyria, Babylon, and Persia great banquets were considered to be an important means of demonstrating the glory of kings. When Ashurnasirpal II dedicated his new capital city of Calah in 879 B.C., he claimed to have 69,574 guests at a banquet. Persian monarchs frequently had as many as 15,000 guests at daily feasts. There were 10,000 guests at the marriage feast of Alexander the Great.[13]

---

12. Ibid., p. 200.
13. Cited in John F. Walvoord, *Daniel: The Key to Prophetic Revelation* (Chicago: Moody, 1971), p. 117.

5:2. He gave orders to bring the gold and silver vessels . . . in order that the king and his nobles, his wives, and his concubines might drink from them. By way of contrast, Nebuchadnezzar at least had enough respect for the God of Israel to place His sacred vessels "into the treasure-house of his god" (1:2). Daniel explained to him that it was this expression of pride and blasphemy that caused the handwriting to appear on the wall and the judgment to be pronounced (5:22-24). That Belshazzar was fully aware of what he was doing to the God of Israel seems implied by his question to Daniel (5:13).

2. *The Handwriting on the Wall* (5:5-12)

5:5. The fingers of a man's hand emerged and began writing opposite the lampstand. Even apart from any human representative or instrument, the Lord was able to vindicate His name and the holiness of Israel's sacred vessels. Compare the fate of the god Dagon in the temple of Ashdod (1 Sam. 5:1-5). Joyce Baldwin's attempt to eliminate the supernatural element in the handwriting on the wall (in an otherwise basically conservative commentary) is both shocking and unconvincing.

On the plaster of the wall of the king's palace. "In the ruins of Nebuchadnezzar's palace archaeologists have uncovered a large throne room 56 feet wide and 173 feet long which probably was the scene of this banquet. Midway in the long wall opposite the entrance there was a niche in front of which the king may well have been seated. Interestingly, the wall behind the niche was covered with white plaster as described by Daniel, which would make an excellent background for such a writing."[14]

5:7. Any man who can read this inscription and explain its interpretation to me will . . . have authority as third ruler in the kingdom. The expression "third ruler in the kingdom" occurs also in verses 16 and 29. There has been considerable debate on the exact meaning of the Aramaic term "third" (*talti*), in view

14. Walvoord, p. 120, citing Koldewey.

of the fact that the normal word for "third" would be *t̲elītāi* (as in 2:39). It has been suggested that it means *triumvir,* that is, one who rules with two others. In any case, it strongly implies that Belshazzar was not the supreme ruler of Babylonia at this time and thus could not make Daniel the second ruler next to himself as Pharaoh did for Joseph (Gen. 41:37-45). Negative critics, of course, are anxious to evaporate the idea of "third" from the word *taltî* because their presuppositions would be honored if the book of Daniel were in error in making Belshazzar the sole ruler of Babylonia. In his *Grammar of Biblical Aramaic,* however, Franz Rosenthal translates the term "one-third (ruler), triumvir."[15]

5:10. The queen entered the banquet hall. Who is this queen? In view of the obvious dignity of this lady and her detailed knowledge of Daniel and of Nebuchadnezzar (whom she calls Belshazzar's "father" three times in verse 11), it seems impossible that it could be Belshazzar's own queen. It could have been *Nitocris,* his mother, a daughter of Nebuchadnezzar (and wife of Nàbonidus; see discussion under 5:1). But in view of the fact that her husband, Nabonidus, had been away from Babylon for so many years and was in disfavor there, this interpretation creates some problems. It seems that the best view is to identify this queen as Amytis, the aged widow of Nebuchadnezzar, for whom he had built the hanging gardens in order that she might not be overly homesick for the hills of her native Media.

3. *The Interpretation of the Writing* (5:13-28)

5:13. Are you that Daniel who is one of the exiles from Judah? It seems highly unlikely that Belshazzar had never personally seen Daniel before. But men do have an amazing ability to ignore completely the things that do not interest them (e.g., Saul, who was so insensitive to spiritual leaders and movements in Israel that he had never even heard of the prophet Samuel! 1 Samuel 9:6-21).

15. Franz Rosenthal, *A Grammar of Biblical Aramaic* (Wiesbaden: Otto Harrassowitz, 1961), pp. 13, 33, 58.

After the death of Nebuchadnezzar, Daniel may have been demoted from his high position. Thus, instead of referring to him as "chief governor over all the wise men of Babylon" (2:48), Belshazzar speaks of him simply as "one of the exiles of Judah, whom my father the king brought from Judah." Perhaps Belshazzar himself had demoted him; but now, in the hour of his deepest need, and through the urgings of his (grand)mother, he calls upon Daniel's reputed skills as an interpreter of dreams.

Why did Belshazzar call him "Daniel" instead of "Belteshazzar," which was his official Babylonian name? The answer could well be that he wanted to emphasize Daniel's humble Jewish background and thereby excuse his own failure to have honored him previously. Also, he may have sought "to avoid the name Belteshazzar which was so similar to his own."[16]

5:17. Keep your gifts for yourself, or give your rewards to someone else; however, I will read the inscription to the king. Daniel was not speaking disrespectfully to Belshazzar (though it is obvious from verses 22-23 that he must have had very little personal respect for this monarch). Rather he was assuring him that no prospect of material gain will deter him from speaking the absolute, divine truth. Daniel realized that the king thought of him as a mere court magician who could be bribed by princely rewards and honors into obtaining a favorable decree from the gods. But after he did fulfill his promise to interpret the handwriting faithfully, he accepted the rewards, doubtless emphasizing that it was the God of Israel, not Daniel the prophet, who provided the interpretation (5:29; cf. 2:28-30).

5:23. But the God in whose hand are your life-breath and your ways, you have not glorified. In spite of his depraved nature and warped personality, Belshazzar, like all men, possessed the image of God indelibly stamped upon his soul. It was his responsibility to glorify God in every area of his life. But he willfully rejected the spiritual message God provided through the

---

16. Edward J. Young, *The Prophecy of Daniel* (Grand Rapids: Eerdmans, 1949), p. 123.

seven years of insanity his (grand)father Nebuchadnezzar experienced (5:22). In fact, Belshazzar went far beyond the boundary lines of his own conscience in committing sacrilege with the sacred vessels of Israel's God (5:23). Therefore his judgment and doom were sealed. No pardon was available at all (contrast 4:27 for Nebuchadnezzar), for his conscience had become hopelessly seared, and his heart was judicially hardened.

5:26. This is the interpretation of the message: "MENE"— God has numbered your kingdom and put an end to it. MENE is a form of the Aramaic "to number." It appears twice for emphasis (compare the doubling of Pharaoh's dream, Gen. 41:32) and like the following two words is a passive participle. H. C. Leupold explains that "there is a kind of double meaning in the verb 'to number.' It means not only 'to count,' but 'to fix the limit of,' as is also the case in our common expression that a man's days are 'numbered.' "[17] Thus, even as God permitted the Amorites to survive until their iniquity was "full" (Gen. 15:16), so the total number of days allotted to the morally rotten Neo-Babylonian kingdom had been reached.

5:27. "TEKEL"—you have been weighed on the scales and found deficient. TEKEL is a form of the Aramaic "to weigh." The Egyptian Book of the Dead pictured men being weighed in balances after death to determine whether their sins outweighed their worthy deeds. But Scripture makes it plain that salvation is never determined that way, for none are worthy (Rom. 3:23). Nevertheless, men *are* weighed by God to determine degrees of reward or punishment (1 Sam. 2:3; Job 31:6; Ps. 62:9; Prov. 16:2).

5:28. "PERES"—your kingdom has been divided and given over to the Medes and Persians. PERES, from the Aramaic "to divide," is the word that actually appeared on the wall rather than *UPHARSIN* (5:25). The latter form has the con-

---

17. H. C. Leupold, *Exposition of Daniel* (Columbus: Wartburg, 1949), p. 234.

junction *U* added, and also the plural ending *IN.* Furthermore, no vowels were included in the mysterious inscription, so that it probably appeared like this: *MN'MN'TKLPRS* (except that it would have been written from right to left as in Hebrew). So terse and enigmatic is this arrangement of words, that it is little wonder that the Babylonian wise men could not interpret it, even if they did understand Aramaic.

The handwriting on the wall spelled doom not only to Belshazzar and his kingdom but also to modern negative critics of this inspired Scripture. Such writers have long insisted that the book of Daniel is guilty of serious historical blunders, especially in presenting the Medes rather than the Persians as the conquerors of Babylon (simply because Darius the *Mede* is said to have received the kingdom, 5:31).

But the handwriting on the wall presents a *dual* monarchy ("the Medes and Persians," 5:28) as the divine instrument of Babylon's destruction. Even more important, the emphasis is clearly upon *Persians* rather than Medes, for the word *PERES* that appeared on the wall was identical to the word *PARAS* (the vowels did not appear), thus providing the double meaning of "Persians" and "divided."

Thus, the book of Daniel does *not* endorse the erroneous idea that it was the Medes that conquered Babylon. This very important point will be developed further as we proceed into the sixth chapter.

4. *The Consequences of the Feast* (5:29-31)

5:30. That same night Belshazzar the Chaldean king was slain. See explanatory comments at 5:1.

5:31. So Darius the Mede received the kingdom at about the age of sixty-two. Who was this ruler? Negative biblical scholarship of our day insists that he was a mere figment of imagination, concocted out of a conglomeration of historical errors in the mind of an unknown writer in the second century B.C. But we may be perfectly sure that God permits no such errors and historical blunders in His infallible Word. "All Scripture is inspired by God and profitable for teaching" (2 Tim. 3:16).

Professor H. H. Rowley of England labored mightily to destroy the confidence of Christians in the historicity of Darius the Mede. He concluded his volume on *Darius the Mede and the Four World Empires of the Book of Daniel* by assuring his readers that, in spite of all the errors, God still speaks through the book of Daniel. "Its very historical mistakes," he wrote, "add to the fullness of its religious message to our hearts, for the God who maketh the wrath of men to praise Him can also convert the mistakes of His servants, whose hearts are consecrated to His service, to rich use."[18] Similarly, Norman W. Porteous was confident that "the witness of the book is important, not in spite of, but precisely because of its limitations in time and circumstance. It can still inspire and instruct us, because it mirrors the faith of men who believed and endured in a definite situation which determined their limited perspective."[19]

Many prominent authors in modern Old Testament scholarship have thus rejected the historicity of major portions of the book of Daniel. But our Lord Jesus Christ exhibited a totally different attitude when He rebuked two disciples on the road to Emmaus: "O foolish men and slow of heart *to believe in all that the prophets have spoken!*" (Luke 24:25). Our Lord made absolutely no distinctions between historical truth in the Old Testament and so-called "religious truth," for religious realities are solidly grounded in Scripture upon historical realities.

Is this "Darius the Mede" ("the son of Ahasuerus, of Median descent," 9:1), then, a confusion for Darius I, a Persian king who reigned a generation later (521-486 B.C.), who was the father of Ahasuerus, that is, Xerxes? The answer is an emphatic no! As Raymond Dougherty so carefully demonstrated, the book of Daniel contains information about the reign of Belshazzar that only the recently discovered cuneiform documents reveal. Only this book, of all ancient books, tells us that Nebuchadnezzar built Babylon himself. And so the critics

---

18. H. H. Rowley, *Darius the Mede and the Four World Empires of the Book of Daniel* (Cardiff: U. of Wales, 1935), p. 182.
19. Porteous, p. 173.

must concede that the author of Daniel was not only "brilliant" but also had access to sources of information that have not been available for nearly two and a half millenniums.[20]

Instead of Darius I of Persia, the book of Daniel is speaking of an entirely different person, a subordinate of Cyrus the Great, who "was made king over the kingdom of the Chaldeans" (9:1, where the verb *homlak,* "was made king," is passive). This can be none other than *Gubaru,* the man whom Cyrus made to be governor over all of Babylonia, who is said in the "Nabonidus Chronicle" to have "installed sub-governors in Babylon."[21] From 535 to 525 B.C., the name *Gubaru* appears frequently in cuneiform texts as the "governor of Babylon and the Region Beyond the River," exercising almost kingly powers in this vast domain covering all of Babylonia, Syria, and Palestine (the entire "Fertile Crescent") during the prolonged absence of his administrative superior, Cyrus the Great (539-530 B.C.).

For a full discussion of Gubaru's identification with Darius the Mede of the book of Daniel, see *Darius the Mede: The Historical Chronology of Daniel.*[22] As in the case of Belshazzar, the final monarch of Babylon, the true identity of Darius the Mede is emerging from the dust of time. In due time, God is graciously vindicating His Word, including the amazing book of Daniel.

20. Pfeiffer, pp. 758-59, 766, 772.
21. Translated by A. Leo Oppenheim in Pritchard, p. 306. See additional comments on GU-BA-RU at 6:28 and note 12.
22. By John C. Whitcomb (Phillipsburg, N.J.: Presbyterian and Reformed, 1959).

6

DANIEL IN THE LIONS' DEN

E. DARIUS'S DECREE (6:1-28)

1. The Prominence of Daniel (6:1-3)

6:1. It seemed good to Darius to appoint 120 satraps over the kingdom, that they should be in charge of the whole kingdom. Once again, critics insist that they have found a historical blunder in the book of Daniel. The ancient Greek historian Herodotus (III, 89) states that Darius I divided the empire into only twenty *satrapies*. So, we are told, the author of the book of Daniel must have been thinking of the 127 provinces in the days of King Xerxes, son of Darius I (Esther 1:1).

But one look at the biblical text reveals that it is the critics who have committed the blunder at this point. The book of Daniel says nothing of "satrapies" or "provinces." It states that 120 "satraps" were set over the kingdom, namely, "the kingdom of the Chaldeans" (9:1). A "satrap" was a Persian official who could rule over a large province or over a small group of people.[1] This would harmonize well with the "Nabonidus Chronicle," which states that Gubaru installed sub-governors in Babylon immediately after the fall of the city to the armies of Cyrus.

Thus, the statement of Daniel 6:1 has nothing whatsoever to do with the division of the Medo-Persian empire into satrapies or provinces that took place during the later administrations of Darius I and Xerxes.

---

1. Robert Dick Wilson, *Studies in the Book of Daniel* (New York: Knickerbocker, 1917), 1:175-78.

6:3. Then this Daniel began distinguishing himself among the commissioners and satraps because he possessed an extraordinary spirit. Babylon had collapsed, and its king was dead. But Daniel continued into the new kingdom. In fact, the new administration of Medo-Persia highly honored him, having heard no doubt of his interpretation of the handwriting on the wall, which pronounced doom upon Belshazzar. Thus, even though the last kings of Babylon and most of the Babylonians (and probably many complacent Israelites in the exile as well) had ignored Daniel for many years, God, in His marvelous providence, saw to it that His faithful prophet received the honor that was due him.

Daniel actually became the third ruler in the former territories of Neo-Babylonia (under Darius the Mede and Cyrus the Great), even as he was belatedly elevated to that same position under Belshazzar and Nabonidus. In similar fashion, Jeremiah was honored by the Babylonians after the fall of Jerusalem, for they had doubtless heard of his many prophetic messages that had announced the imminent fall of Jerusalem to the Babylonians, and for which he had suffered greatly at the hands of the Jews. As a reward, they gave him the choice of luxurious living in Babylon or an honorable position in Judah under Gedaliah the governor, plus a portion of food and a gift (Jer. 39:11-14; 40:1-6).

2. *The Plot Against Daniel* (6:4-9)

6:7. All the commissioners of the kingdom . . . have consulted together. In view of the fact that these two commissioners lied to Darius the Mede in claiming that Daniel had consulted with them, it is highly probable that many if not most of the 120 satraps were likewise ignorant of this cunning plot. (See note on verse 24.)

Anyone who makes a petition to any god or man besides you, O king, for thirty days. It has been objected that such a decree would have been utterly impossible to enforce and is therefore fictitious. But it must be recognized that the phrase "makes a petition to any god or man" has reference not to the ordinary requests of daily life but rather to prayers only. Even James A. Montgomery, by no means an orthodox scholar, states that "G. Behrmann's position is an entirely sensible one, that the implication of the story means a petition of religion (not, with A. A. Bevan, any kind of request), and that this one king was to be regarded for the time being as the only representative of Deity."[2]

The sixth chapter of Daniel clearly indicates that the decree was not the product of calm and calculating reflection on the part of Darius the Mede. On the contrary, it was foisted upon the unsuspecting monarch by a group of men who would never have conceived of such a fantastic proclamation had they not been overwhelmed by their jealousy of Daniel.

"Of course there is difficulty in the account," wrote Edward J. Young, "but who is to say that an oriental despot, yielding to the subtle flattery of such a proposal, might not, in a weak moment, have agreed to it?"[3] Darius himself no doubt realized too late that he had been led into a trap. But the very fact that such a decree had been prepared and signed shows how deeply ingrained were the polytheisms of the ancient world and how attractive were the pharaoh-worshiping customs of Egypt that soon came into shocking fruition in the Hellenistic age after the conquests of Alexander the Great.

Shall be cast into the lions' den. The official form of execution under Darius the Mede is said to be "the lions' den," whereas in the days of Nebuchadnezzar it had been the "furnace of blazing fire" (Dan. 3; cf. Jer. 29:22). The historical significance of this change is that the state religion of Medo-Persia, namely, Zoroastrianism, involved the worship of Atar the fire-god.[4] Thus, for the Medo-Persians to have used a fur-

2. James A. Montgomery, *A Critical and Exegetical Commentary on the Book of Daniel,* The International Critical Commentary (Edinburgh: T. & T. Clark, 1927), p. 270. See also S. R. Driver, *The Book of Daniel* (Cambridge: Cambridge U., 1900), p. 73.
3. Edward J. Young, *Exposition of Daniel* (Columbus: Wartburg, 1949), p. 133.
4. A. T. Olmstead, *The History of the Persian Empire* (Chicago: U. of Chicago, 1948), p. 473.

nace of fire as a means for destroying criminals would have appeared sacrilegious. Such details, introduced quite incidentally into the narrative, provide further confirmation of the historicity of the sixth chapter of Daniel.

6:8. The law of the Medes and Persians, which may not be revoked. Just as the handwriting on the wall had revealed the imminent collapse of Babylon under the blows of a *dual* monarchy, with the emphasis on *Persia,* so also in this chapter it is clear that the critical views of the origin of the book of Daniel can only be maintained by ignoring the clear statements of the text. Darius the Mede is not presented here as the supreme monarch of a Median empire but as a Mede who ruled Babylon under "the law of the Medes *and Persians.*"

The book of Daniel is accurate in listing the Medes first because, in spite of the fact that the emperor, Cyrus, was a Persian, the bulk of his army at this time was still Median. Only a dozen years earlier he had conquered and absorbed the numerically superior Median army of the aging and corrupt King Astyages (550 B.C.) into a new and vastly superior Medo-Persian military unit. Two generations later, however, the Persian domination of the Medes had become almost complete, so that in the days of king Xerxes (486-65 B.C.) the Persian element could be mentioned first (Esther 1:19, etc., though not in 10:2).

This was a law "which may not be revoked." Not even the king in Medo-Persia had the power to change a royal decree, and this could sometimes create great frustration, as depicted in the book of Esther (8:8). That is the main reason the Medo-Persian form of government was "inferior" to that of Nebuchadnezzar, the absolute dictator of Neo-Babylonia, whose slightest word was law. The head of gold had thus given way to arms of silver (Dan. 2:38-39).

Apart from Scripture (Dan. 6:8, 12, 15; Esther 1:19; 8:8), the function of such a law cannot be clearly illustrated. Carey A. Moore is among the many negative critics who would maintain that "there is no evidence for this irrevocability of the Persian law. . . . Certainly such a law seems inflexible and crippling to good government, and, hence, improbable."[5]

It seems quite surprising, however, in the light of such comments, that Old Testament scholars have not given more attention to the incident recorded by Diodorus Siculus, a second-century B.C. historian, concerning Darius III (335-31 B.C.), who, in a great rage, condemned a certain Charidemus to death. Later, however, "when the king's anger abated, he at once repented and blamed himself for having made the greatest mistake, but . . . it was not possible for what was done by the royal authority to be undone" (Grk: *all' ou gar ēn dunaton to gegonos dia tēs basilikēs exousias agenēton kataskeuasai*).[6]

If this means merely that Charidemus could not be brought back from the dead, it would be, in the words of J. Stafford Wright, "a piece of sententious moralizing and would not be improved by adding 'by the royal authority.' "[7] Furthermore, "the use here of the perfect participle (*to gegonos,* "what was done") and the adjective (*basilikēs,* "royal") makes the statement a general comment on Persian law"[8] instead of a mere personal experience of Darius III, especially when "the law of the Persians" is referred to about ten lines earlier.

Thus, we have in a pre-Christian historian a rather clear testimony to the existence to the kind of Medo-Persian law referred to in Daniel and Esther. The self-authenticating Word of God does not need such secular confirmation to be believed; but we appreciate God's providential provision of background information for biblical events.

3. *The Prayer of Daniel* (6:10)

(a) Toward Jerusalem. Daniel took very seriously the dedicatory prayer of Solomon at the completion of the great Temple in Jerusalem. In this prayer, Solomon anticipated the

---

5. Carey A. Moore, *Esther,* The Anchor Bible (Garden City, N.Y.: Doubleday, 1971), p. 11.
6. J. Stafford Wright, "The Historicity of Esther," in J. Barton Payne, ed., *New Perspectives on the Old Testament* (Waco, Tex.: Word, 1970), p. 39.
7. Wright, p. 40.
8. Ibid. See also John C. Whitcomb, *Esther: Triumph of God's Sovereignty* (Chicago: Moody, 1979), pp. 40-42.

day when God's people would be in a land of captivity and would repent of their sins. Under such circumstances, "if they return to Thee with all their heart and with all their soul in the land of their enemies . . . and pray to Thee toward their land which Thou hast given to their fathers, the city which Thou hast chosen . . . then hear their prayer and . . . maintain their cause" (1 Kings 8:46-50).

Daniel knew that even though Jerusalem and its beautiful Temple had been destroyed, it was still the theocratic center of the earth. In fact, even the very hours of his prayers were determined by the hours of sacrifice in the Temple, though all such sacrifices had ended years earlier (see 9:21). Jonah likewise promised, in an hour of utter desperation, to "look again toward Thy holy temple" (2:4), even though it must have been difficult in his situation to know in which direction to look!

(b) Three times a day. Daniel may well have used David's daily prayer pattern as his own—"evening and morning and at noon, I will complain and murmur, and He will hear my voice" (Ps. 55:17).

(c) Giving thanks before his God. Under such circumstances, one might wonder what there was to be thankful for. But Spirit-filled men in the Old Testament era did not have to have the New Testament to know that "in everything by prayer and supplication with thanksgiving" they were to let their "requests be made known to God" (Phil. 4:6).

(d) As he had been doing previously. The Scriptures make very clear that Daniel did not wait until a crisis came to begin praying to his God. To the contrary, good prayer habits will give us deep confidence in God's providential care no matter what may come. "For he will never be shaken. . . . He will not fear evil tidings; his heart is steadfast, trusting in the Lord. His heart is upheld, he will not fear" (Ps. 112:6-8).

4. *The Condemnation of Daniel* (6:11-17)

6:14. As soon as the king heard this statement, he was deeply distressed. The mighty Darius the Mede was trapped in the snare of his own pride and folly—and he knew it. We need only compare his pitiful plight with that of another great king, who was tricked into beheading John the Baptist: "Although the king was very sorry, yet because of his oaths and because of his dinner guests, he was unwilling to refuse" (Mark 6:26).

Even until sunset he kept exerting himself to rescue him. How great was the difference between Medo-Persian monarchs and Neo-Babylonian monarchs. It was as great as the difference between gold and silver. Could we ever imagine a Nebuchadnezzar laboring "until sunset" to cancel the effects of some arbitrary decree he had previously issued?

Apparently there was a Medo-Persian law that criminals had to be executed the same day as their crime. This would at least have the advantage of preventing the hatching of counter plots to accomplish the rescue of the accused person.

6:16. Your God whom you constantly serve will Himself deliver you. These remarkable words from the lips of Darius the Mede (cf. v. 20) provide a measurement of the impact of Daniel's testimony for his God in the midst of a pagan court.

6:17. And a stone was brought . . . and the king sealed it. Compare the equally futile sealing of the tomb of our Lord (Matt. 27:66).

5. *The Deliverance of Daniel* (6:18-28)

6:22. My God sent His angel and shut the lions' mouths, and they have not harmed me. When God delivers supernaturally, He does a complete work. Daniel's three friends had already discovered this in Nebuchadnezzar's furnace. Darius the Mede did not hear the plaintive cry of a man half eaten by lions. Not only were the lions' mouths shut by the Lord, but their very natures may have been subdued, as during the Flood in Noah's ark and during the coming Kingdom age, when "the lion will eat straw like the ox" (Isa. 11:7; 65:25; see also Ezek. 34:25; Hosea 2:18). Daniel may well have thought also of the poetic picture of a righteous man in the book of Job: "Neither will

you be afraid of wild beasts . . . for the beasts of the field will
be at peace with you" (Job 5:22-23). Daniel's trust in God is
enshrined also within a great New Testament chapter: "who by
faith . . . shut the mouths of lions" (Heb. 11:33).

*6:23. No injury whatever was found on him, because he had
trusted in his God.* Compare the complete deliverance of
Daniel's three friends (3:27) and, even earlier, of the prophet
Jeremiah (Jer. 38:11-13).

*6:24. They brought those men who had maliciously accused
Daniel.* It seems unlikely that 122 men plus their families would
have been thrown into this lions' den (120 satraps and two of
the three commissioners). It is probable that only a handful of
men had engineered this plot and were therefore executed for
their wickedness. Nevertheless, ancient kings, like modern
ones, were capable of extreme and irrational acts of violence.

*They cast them, their children, and their wives into the lions'
den.* The God of Israel gave a law to His people through Moses
that children should not "be put to death for their fathers;
everyone shall be put to death for his own sin" (Deut. 24:16;
cf. 2 Kings 14:6). If Achan's entire family was stoned to death
for his sin, it was because all of them were active participants
with the head of the household in this particular sin (Josh.
7:24-26).

But the Medo-Persians had no such merciful law. Wives,
children, and other relatives were often killed at the king's
command when a man committed a serious crime against the
royal house, thus "nipping in the bud" any possible retaliation
by the criminal's family (to say nothing of the deterrent that
such drastic justice would provide for potential enemies). The
Greek historian Herodotus presents one clear example of this
form of royal justice (Book III, 119).

*6:28. So this Daniel enjoyed success in the reign of Darius and
in the reign of Cyrus the Persian.* Negative critics have long insisted that this statement proves the historical incompetence of

the author of the book of Daniel. They understand it to mean that an independent Median empire under Darius was followed by the conquests of Cyrus the Persian. Such a sequence of events, of course, never happened, and thus the author supposedly committed a serious blunder, betraying, therefore, the late date of the book.

The critical view is utterly impossible for a number of reasons, the greatest being that our Lord Jesus Christ endorsed the authenticity of the book of Daniel and thus asserted its authority as the inerrant Word of God. In His appeal to this great book, He stated: "Let the reader understand" (Matt. 24:15). In addition to this, the book of Daniel itself denies the system that has been imposed upon it (see comments on 5:28 and 6:8).

Another interpretation of this statement, proposed by the British evangelical scholar Donald J. Wiseman, is that the conjunction "and" should be understood as an explicative, "even," *thus identifying Darius with Cyrus* (see 1 Chron. 5:26 for an example of such a rendering).[9] But it is difficult to understand how a contemporary writer could have been referring to *Cyrus the Persian, son of Cambyses,* when he wrote of a man who was *the son of Ahasuerus, of the seed of the Medes.*[10] Furthermore, as has already been pointed out, Darius the Mede was made king of Babylonia (9:1), not simply by God (which would be true of all rulers) but by a more powerful human ruler, namely, Cyrus the Great.[11]

An additional problem with the equating of Darius the Mede with Cyrus the Persian is illustrated in the commentary on this chapter by Joyce Baldwin, who accepts Wiseman's view. She describes Darius the Mede as a ruler who needed the decree of Daniel 6:6-9 "to boost his ego and give expression to his new

9. Donald J. Wiseman, ed., *Notes on Some Problems in the Book of Daniel* (London: Tyndale, 1965), p. 14.
10. John C. Whitcomb, *Darius the Mede: The Historical Chronology of Daniel* (Phillipsburg, N.J.: Presbyterian and Reformed, 1959), pp. 46-49.
11. John C. Whitcomb, "Cyrus in the Prophecies of Isaiah," in John H. Skilton, ed., *The Law and the Prophets* (Phillipsburg, N.J.: Presbyterian and Reformed, 1974), pp. 388-401.

authority" because he was an "inexperienced king" (p. 128). But this clearly contradicts the biblical and historical evidence of Cyrus's great previous conquests of the Median and Lydian empires (cf. Isa. 45:1-7; Dan. 7:5).

Although Wiseman's view has been accepted by some British scholars, in North America there seems to be a preference for equating Darius the Mede with Gubaru the Governor of Babylon and the Region Beyond the River (e.g., Gleason L. Archer, R. K. Harrison, and Horace D. Hummel). This means that Daniel 6:28 refers to two distinct rulers, Darius the Mede being subordinate to and contemporary with Cyrus the Great.[12]

In this day of vast spiritual apostasy and pseudointellectualism, the book of Daniel stands as a mighty rock of inspired prophetic Scripture, totally unshaken by the seemingly endless attacks of critics. May we, as servants of the same God whom Daniel knew, seek His help in reading this precious book with the understanding that He alone can fully provide.

---

12. Cf. Gleason L. Archer, "Daniel," in Frank E. Gaebelein, ed., *The Expositor's Bible Commentary* (Grand Rapids: Zondervan, 1985) 7:76-77; Roland K. Harrison, *Introduction to the Old Testament*, pp. 512, 1122; C. Hassell Bullock, *An Introduction to the Old Testament Prophetic Books* (Chicago: Moody, 1986), pp. 284-85; and Horace D. Hummel, *The Word Becoming Flesh* (St. Louis: Concordia, 1979), p. 563: "most conservatives follow the solution proposed by Whitcomb." However, William H. Shea offers a different perspective on GUBARU. While rejecting Wiseman's view, he makes no distinction between the *Ugbaru* who conquered Babylon and the *Gubaru* who appointed sub-governors in Babylon ("Darius the Mede: An Update," *Andrews University Seminary Studies* 20:3 [Autumn 1982], pp. 229-47; and "A Further Note on Daniel 6: Daniel As 'Governor' " AUSS 21:2 [Summer 1983], pp. 169-71). Shea believes that this Ugbaru/Gubaru *died a year and three weeks after the fall of Babylon* and thus reigned for fourteen months under the title "Darius the Mede" before Cyrus finally assumed the title "King of Babylon." This view deserves careful study. One major difficulty, of course, is that it ignores the clear distinction between the names UG-BA-RU and GU-BA-RU in the cuneiform text of the *Nabonidus Chronicle*. A. K. Grayson *(Assyrian and Babylonian Chronicles* [Locust Valley, N.Y.: J. J. Augustin, 1975] states that in line 15 of this chronicle "the sign UG [in UG-BA-RU] is faint but the reading is certain" (p. 109). He raises no question about the readings GU-BA-RU in line 20 or UG-BA-RU in line 22 (p. 110). Cf. Whitcomb, *Darius the Mede*, pp. 17-20.

7

THE FOUR KINGDOMS
AND THE LITTLE HORN

F. DANIEL'S DREAM OF THE FOUR BEASTS (7:1-27)

1. *Daniel's Vision* (7:1-8)

7:1. In the first year of Belshazzar king of Babylon. The year is
553 B.C. (the kingship of Babylon has just been entrusted to
Belshazzar by his father Nabonidus in the third year of the latter's reign). A half century has now elapsed since Daniel interpreted Nebuchadnezzar's vision of the great four-part image.
Now the mighty Nebuchadnezzar has been dead for ten years,
and his successors upon the throne of Babylon have been incomparably weaker, leading the kingdom to inevitable disaster.

The historical section of the book of Daniel (chapters 1-6)
brought us down to about 538 B.C., shortly after the conquest
of Babylon by Medo-Persia. Daniel was delivered from the den
of lions and then "enjoyed success in the reign of Darius and in
the reign of Cyrus the Persian" (6:28).

Now the author begins the last section of his book—the final
four prophetic visions, which concentrate on the destiny of
Israel among the nations—by shifting back in time to the
beginning of the reign of Belshazzar. Within three years Cyrus
would begin his conquest of Media, then Lydia in Asia Minor,
and finally Babylon. Thus, the handwriting of doom for Belshazzar's kingdom is already being prepared upon the horizon
of history.

There are remarkable similarities between the vision of
chapter 7 that Daniel saw one night and the one Nebuchadnez-

zar had seen back in 603 B.C. Both visions provided a four-plus-one system of prophecy. Nebuchadnezzar had seen an image of *gold* (Babylon), *silver* (Medo-Persia), *bronze* (the Hellenistic empire of Alexander the Great), and *iron* (Rome), which was then followed by the fifth and final kingdom, the *stone* kingdom of Messiah (Christ), the Son of God, who smashed the entire image and replaced it with His own divine, eternal, holy, perfect kingdom—a kingdom as brilliant as a diamond—four-plus-one.

Now in the seventh chapter we find exactly the same pattern, but in a significantly different form—wild animals instead of well-shaped and polished metals.

Furthermore, in both visions we see a *duality* in the second kingdom. Chapter 2 depicts this second kingdom, Medo-Persia, in the form of two arms of silver. Chapter 7 also depicts this duality, but again, in a different form.

Finally, in both visions we find a ten-fold division in the fourth kingdom. In chapter 2 this is symbolized by ten toes on the feet of the image, whereas in the seventh chapter it is ten horns on the head of a great monster.

The *similarities* are highly significant, for they emphasize the great importance of God's message to Israel and to the world of mankind concerning the ultimate unfolding of history. God had given to Pharaoh also two distinct, yet similar, dreams: one of seven cows and one of seven ears of grain. Joseph explained that the "dreams are one and the same; God has told to Pharaoh what He is about to do. . . . Now as for the repeating of the dream to Pharaoh twice, it means that the matter is determined by God, and God will quickly bring it about" (Gen. 41:25, 32).

The *differences* between the two visions are also quite significant: first, and most important, the contrasting perspectives. In chapter 2 we looked up to a mighty monument, magnificent, beautiful, brilliant—an image of purely human achievement in government, culture, art, and science. But in the seventh chapter we see that same fourfold empire of man from God's perspective. And how does it appear? As wild and ravenous beasts! That is how a holy God views the sinful and satanic maneuverings of nations upon the earth. Men's achievements apart from and in opposition to Him are not spectacular from heaven's perspective. In fact, they are far worse than the activities of wild, carnivorous animals, for no animal ever sins, or, for that matter, is ever cruel. What they do is done by genetically programmed instinct patterns that were warped through God's curse upon Adam and his progeny. There is no hell for the animal kingdom. But men are wicked and cruel in the sight of God and are under His judgment. That is the emphasis of chapter 7.

The other contrast has to do with the tenfold aspect of the fourth kingdom. In the second chapter, man's program ends with ten subdivisions. They are all smashed by the Stone, along with the entire image above them. That is the end. But in chapter 7 we discover that the whole story was not told. After the ten horns are introduced, obviously corresponding to the ten toes, *an eleventh horn* appears, a little one that comes up after them. And the focus of the seventh chapter is not on the ten but rather upon this eleventh horn, which turns out to be none other than the final Antichrist, a masterpiece of Satan, just before the great Stone crashes down from heaven. This little horn epitomizes all that is depraved and demonic in the world system of mankind apart from Jesus Christ the Lord.

7:2. I was looking in my vision by night, and behold, the four winds of heaven were stirring up the great sea. In biblical symbolism, "the great sea" pictures fallen humanity (cf. Isa. 8:6-8; 17:12-13; 57:20; Jer. 6:23; 46:7-8; 47:2; Matt. 13:47; Rev. 13:1; 17:1, 15). "The four winds of heaven" probably speak of the angelic forces through which God controls and moves the nations. "Of more than 120 references in the Bible to wind (more than 90 in the O.T. and about 30 in the N.T.), well over half are related to events and ideas which reflect the sovereignty and power of God."[1]

---

1. John F. Walvoord, *Daniel: The Key to Prophetic Revelation* (Chicago: Moody, 1971), p. 152.

7:3. And four great beasts were coming up from the sea. As the interpreting angel soon explains to Daniel, "these great beasts . . . are four kings who will arise from the earth" (7:17). They clearly correspond to the four kingdoms predicted in Daniel 2 and are represented as four distinct metals in the image.

7:4. The first was like a lion and had the wings of an eagle. Jeremiah had spoken of Nebuchadnezzar as "a lion from the thickets of the Jordan" (Jer. 49:19; 50:44), for when the Jordan River overflowed its banks in the spring, lions were driven from its thickets and attacked people in surrounding villages (cf. Prov. 22:13; 26:13). Nebuchadnezzar is described as having "the wings of an eagle" because his armies could move with great speed to conquer enemies (Ezek. 17:3, 7), as Pharaoh Necho discovered to his horror after the Battle of Carchemish (605 B.C.; see comments on 1:2).

Its wings were plucked, and it was . . . made to stand on two feet like a man; a human mind also was given to it. Nebuchadnezzar, under God's chastening hand, had his pride removed from him like feathers from a bird and was made to look utterly insane until he repented and surrendered to the God of Israel (Dan. 4). It was probably the spiritual transformation God accomplished within him that is here symbolized by the beast's nature being transformed into a human nature (see discussion at 4:37).

7:5. A second [beast] resembling a bear . . . was raised up on one side, and three ribs were in its mouth. This is an apt description of the Medo-Persian empire under Cyrus and Cambyses and corresponds to the two silver arms of the image of Daniel 2. A bear is less majestic and swift than a lion. The final Antichrist is depicted as a beast with feet "like those of a bear" (Rev. 13:2). The additional detail, not depicted in the arms, is the lopsided character of this empire, with Median influence being predominate during the reigns of Cyrus and Cambyses (see comments on 5:28; 6:8; and 8:3) but shifting to Persian dominance by the time of Xerxes fifty years later (Esther 1:19, "the laws of the Persians and the Medes").

The three ribs in the mouth of the monstrous bear probably refer to the three greatest conquests of the Medo-Persians under Cyrus and his son Cambyses: (1) Lydia in Asia Minor under King Croesus, 546 B.C.; (2) Babylon under Nabonidus and Belshazzar, 539 B.C.; and (3) Egypt under Psamtik III, 525 B.C.

7:6. Another [beast] like a leopard . . . had on its back four wings of a bird . . . four heads, and dominion was given to it. Again, we find a perfectly appropriate correspondence with the belly and thighs of bronze in chapter 2. The kingdom of Alexander the Great grew with almost incomparable speed, so that a short ten years after he invaded Asia Minor (334 B.C.), he had conquered the entire Medo-Persian empire under Darius III including Syria, Palestine, Egypt, and the eastern territories to the borders of India, and then died at the age of thirty-three. If Nebuchadnezzar conquered swiftly (two wings), Alexander exceeded him (four wings). Frequently in the Old Testament, leopards depict that which is terrifying (Jer. 5:6; Hos. 13:7; Hab. 1:8). For further discussion of Alexander's kingdom, see 8:5-8.

The fact that this beast is shown with "four heads" (compare its "four wings of a bird") points to the four major divisions of Alexander's empire following his death in 323 B.C.: (1) Babylon and north Syria under Antigonus (later under Seleucus I Nicator); (2) Egypt under Ptolemy I Soter; (3) Macedonia under Cassander; and (4) Thrace and Bithynia under Lysimachus. Compare comments on 8:8 and 11:4.[2]

7:7. Behold, a fourth beast, dreadful and terrifying and extremely strong; and it had large iron teeth . . . and it was dif-

2. James L. Boyer, "Chart of the Period Between the Testaments" (Winona Lake, Ind.: BMH Books, 1962), with discussion of source materials, and chronology based on Richard A. Parker and Waldo H. Dubberstein, *Babylonian Chronology 626 B.C.-A.D. 75* (Providence, R.I.: Brown U., 1956). See also Raymond F. Surburg, *Introduction to the Intertestamental Period* (St. Louis: Concordia, 1975).

ferent from all the beasts that were before it, and it had ten horns. Not only does this beast produce ten subdivisions (as the feet of the image in Daniel 2), but the same metallic substance is involved as well: *iron.*

The identification of this kingdom as Rome can hardly be questioned except by those whose presuppositions do not permit them to believe in the possibility of predictive prophecy. Rome did not enter the scene of Palestine as a crushing force until 63 B.C., when the Roman general Pompey captured Jerusalem. Since the book of Daniel *had* to be written long before that date (see Introduction), we are locked into the realm of predictive prophecy as we contemplate these astonishing words. This "dreadful and terrifying" kingdom of iron outlasted all the others combined and conquered vastly more territory than its predecessors.

7:8. Behold, another horn, a little one, came up among them, and . . . possessed eyes like the eyes of a man, and a mouth uttering great boasts. This is a spectacular new element in predictive prophecy, only faintly hinted at in the writing prophets that preceded Daniel (Isa. 27:1, "the dragon who lives in the sea"). Christ and the apostles referred to this person as yet future to their own time (Matt. 24:5, 15; 2 Thess. 2:3-4; 1 John 2:18; 4:3; Rev. 13; 17; 19). The fact that he is said to come up "among" the ten horns indicates, therefore, that these horns (kings) are also yet future to the New Testament era. Frequently in the Old Testament the term *horn* is used to describe power, and thus, appropriately, powerful rulers (1 Kings 22:11; Ps. 75:10; 132:17; Zech. 1:18).

"Eyes like the eyes of a man" suggests great brilliance (cf. Ezek. 1; Zech. 3:9; 4:10); the "mouth uttering great boasts," in the light of later revelation, refers to blasphemous utterances (7:25; Rev. 13:5-6). The combination of these two characteristics points to a man capable of incomparably brilliant blasphemies, not simply speaking against God but doing so in a manner that will attract and deceive vast numbers of men. Indeed, he will be Satan's masterpiece—a superbly effective instrument of "the father of lies," who was "a murderer from the beginning" (John 8:44).

Three of the first horns were pulled out by the roots before it.
The interpreting angel amplifies this statement in verse 20
("before which three of them fell") and in verse 24 ("and will
subdue three kings"). The threefold emphasis on this event
(revealed nowhere else in prophetic Scripture) indicates a
crucial means for Israel's future identification of the "little
horn." Somehow, this powerful king will rise rapidly to international prominence by utterly crushing three of the ten kings
who will already be on the scene (analogous to the three ribs in
the mouth of the second beast, v. 5).

2. *The Ancient of Days* (7:9-15)

A greater contrast between two connecting verses can hardly
be imagined. In verses 7 and 8 we see the frightful fourth beast
with its blasphemous little horn. This is the devil at his worst.
Then, with hardly a word of transition, the reader is hurried
into the third heaven, into the very presence of God, where
everything is under His absolutely sovereign control. "He who
sits in the heavens laughs, the Lord scoffs at them. Then He
will speak unto them in His anger and terrify them in His fury"
(Ps. 2:4-5). The only possible outcome of this confrontation in
a God-created moral universe is utter and final divine judgment
on every form of rebellion and wickedness.

7:9. The Ancient of Days took His seat. In the light of verse 13,
this divine being seems to be God the Father, for "a Son of
Man" approaches Him to receive the kingdom. The picture of
snow-white vesture, white "hair," flaming "throne," burning
"wheels," "a river of fire . . . coming out from before Him"
(see Ps. 97:3; Rev. 1:14-15), "myriads [ten thousands] upon
myriads standing before Him" (Deut. 33:2), and "the books
opened" (cf. Rev. 20:12) provides overpowering impressions
of the glory and holiness and power and greatness of our God.
We can understand why men who caught a mere glimpse of
God's glory would fall at His feet as dead (Rev. 1:17). In God's
presence, Paul "heard inexpressible words" (2 Cor. 12:4) and
as a result received a "thorn in the flesh" to prevent pride from
such an experience.

7:11. I kept looking . . . until the beast was slain. A confrontation between the despicable fourth beast and the infinite Ancient of Days surely could not continue long in Daniel's vision.
The fact that it continues for centuries in the real world is a major mystery in God's providential rule. The fiery destruction of
the beast corresponds to the smashing of the image in Daniel 2
by means of the Stone from heaven (Rev. 19:20). In both cases,
the end comes suddenly, supernaturally, and spectacularly.

*7:12. As for the rest of the beasts, their dominion was taken
away, but an extension of life was granted to them for an appointed period of time.* There is a significant contrast between
the termination of the dominion of the fourth beast and that of
the first three. As explained in the comments on 2:35, Neo-
Babylonia, Medo-Persia, and Greece were not totally destroyed when they lost their dominion but were largely merged
into succeeding empires, so that elements of each still exist in
the final phase of the Roman kingdom. Totally different, however, will be the fate of the fourth kingdom at the second coming. Nothing of it will be left to contaminate Christ's millennial
kingdom. Then, and then only, will God smash the kingdoms
of this world. They "became like chaff from the summer
threshing floors; and the wind carried them away so that not a
trace of them was found" (2:35).[3]

*7:13. And behold, with the clouds of heaven one like a Son of
Man was coming.* "The clouds of heaven" in this context
speak of deity, as may be seen by comparing 1 Thessalonians
4:17 with Revelation 1:7 and Acts 1:9-11. "Clouds in Scripture
are frequently characteristic of revelation of deity (Ex.
13:21-22; 19:9, 16; 1 Kings 8:10-11; Isa. 19:1; Jer. 4:13; Ezek.
10:4; Matt. 24:30; 26:64; Mark 13:26)."[4]

For many centuries God had been preparing mankind, and
especially the nation of Israel, for the coming of a Redeemer
who would be both divine and human in one person. Beginning
with the cryptic prophecy of the seed of the woman (Gen. 3:15;

3. Walvoord, p. 166.
4. Ibid., p. 167.

Rom. 16:20), narrowing to the seed of Abraham (Gen. 12:3), then the tribe of Judah (Gen. 49:10), and finally the line of David and Solomon (2 Sam. 7:12-16), God brought brilliant light upon His dual nature in the writings of Isaiah (4:2; 7:14; 9:6; 11:1-5, 10; 42:1-8; 49:1-8; 50:4-9; 52:13—53:12).

Although Messiah had already been named as God's "Son" in previous prophetic utterances (cf. Ps. 2:7, 12; Prov. 30:4), He is now given a name that emphasizes His true and total identification with mankind. This is the name that our Lord used most frequently of Himself (thirty-one times in Matthew alone), as if to emphasize the genuineness and permanence of His present humanity in contrast to the frequent but temporary appearances (theophanies) men had observed during His preincarnate state and ministries.[5]

And He came up to the Ancient of Days. This is one of the very few instances in the Old Testament where God the Son is *symbolically* distinguished from God the Father (see comments on 7:9). The event (which follows v. 10 chronologically) is the sovereign bestowal of the kingdom by the Father to the Son at the time of the second coming (cf. Ps. 2:6-9; Luke 19:12-27; Rev. 5).

7:14. And to Him was given dominion, glory and a kingdom . . . which will not be destroyed. By virtue of His authority as Creator of heaven and earth (John 1:3; Col. 1:16; Heb. 1:2), our Lord Jesus Christ deserves to receive the kingdom from the Father. But in addition to this, He paid the full price of our redemption upon the cross, and, in the process, defeated the enemy, Satan (Heb. 2:14). Thus, by double right, creation and redemption, Christ receives an eternal kingdom that no one else deserves to rule. Someday the twenty-four elders will reflect on this as they cry out: "Worthy art Thou, our Lord and our God, to receive glory and honor and power; for Thou

5. Robert D. Rowe, "Is Daniel's 'Son of Man' Messianic?" in Harold H. Rowden, ed., *Christ the Lord* (Downers Grove, Ill.: InterVarsity, 1982), pp. 71-79; and R. T. France, *Jesus and the Old Testament* (Grand Rapids: Baker, 1982).

didst create all things. . . . Worthy art Thou to take the book, and to break its seals; for Thou wast slain . . ." (Rev. 4:11; 5:9).

This kingdom, in its full outward expression, begins on earth at the second coming of Christ, continues for 1,000 years (i.e., the Millennium), and then merges into the eternal state. It will require all eternity for God's servants to begin to learn the fulness of His greatness as "King of kings and Lord of lords" (Rev. 19:16).

> The present church age is not included in the Old Testament prophetic foreviews. The first and second comings of Christ are frequently spoken of in the same breath, as for instance in Isaiah 61:1-2, which Christ expounded in Luke 4:18-19. . . . In a similar way, in his prophetic vision, Daniel takes human history up to the first coming of Christ when the Roman Empire was in sway, and then leaps to the end of the age.[6]

In the meantime, as the ravenous beasts of worldly kingdoms rage against Him and against each other, God's people are being chosen from among the nations (Acts 15:14) and are being prepared to rule and reign with Him (Rev. 20:6) in His coming kingdom. No one, not even the angels of heaven, knows when the kingdom will come, for the date has been fixed by the Father's own authority (Matt. 24:36; Acts 1:7). He knows what Satan's kingdom is accomplishing within His universal and infinite providence, and He knows exactly how and when it will be brought to catastrophic destruction. Such assurance is enormously comforting to His servants in the midst of their afflictions.

7:15. As for me, Daniel, my spirit was distressed within me. God's prophet was not a casual bystander in the special revelation of God to His people. He was deeply and emotionally involved in God's prophetic program, and so must we be. Instead of merely intellectual academic detachment, he was profoundly affected by the overwhelming word of God (see 4:19; 7:28).

6. Walvoord, pp. 169-70.

3. *The Interpretation of the Vision* (7:16-27)

7:16. I approached one of those who were standing by and began asking him the exact meaning of all this. We may be profoundly grateful that Daniel was not satisfied with his visionary prophetic lesson that night. He had an insatiable desire for more and more explanations and interpretations of God's infinitely precious Word, and therefore more truth was given to him and to us by the interpreting angel. How much of His Word would never have been revealed if (on the purely human level) Christ's disciples had never asked questions of their Lord! God invites us to ask Him for wisdom in the interpretation of His Word (James 1:5), with the understanding that He is not obliged to reveal to us all of His "secret things" (Deut. 29:29; John 16:12). Nevertheless, many of God's servants would give a great deal to stand, as it were, in Daniel's shoes and to ask an angelic interpreter "the exact meaning of all this"!

7:17-18. Four kings . . . will arise from the earth. But the saints of the Highest One will receive the kingdom and possess the kingdom forever. The interpreting angel very briefly points to two key ideas. First, these beasts represent human kings and their kingdoms (2:37-44). Second, their dominions will not last forever but will be replaced by God's kingdom, governed through His people, which will indeed continue forever (2:44).

7:19-22. Then I desired to know the exact meaning of the fourth beast . . . the ten horns that were on its head, and the other horn which came up. Because of the similarity of this vision to the one he had interpreted for Nebuchadnezzar a half century earlier, Daniel may have surmised the two key ideas that the angel gave him. Biblical revelation does follow consistent patterns, even in eschatology, so that the careful and reverent interpreter need not be totally frustrated, even by the use of symbolic language.

Encouraged now by the willingness of the angel to help him, Daniel boldly asked for more particulars on the dreadful fourth beast (with "claws of bronze"—a new detail) and its ten horns, but especially that "other horn which came up . . . which was larger in appearance than its associates." But before waiting for the angel's answer, he had to continue describing the fascinating outcome of the great conflict to reassure himself (and us) that however dreadful the earthly kingdoms might be in their wickedness, God is sovereign in the universe, and His mighty program will finally prevail through His people, to whom victory will come in spite of the apparent "overpowering" war waged against them by the little horn (cf. Ps. 110:1-3).

7:24. And another will arise after them, and he will be different from the previous ones and will subdue three kings. The angel, realizing that Daniel was particularly fascinated by the eleventh horn, hurries through his explanation of the fourth beast and its ten horns and reveals a new truth concerning the eleventh horn: it "will arise after" the first ten. It cannot be long after, for Daniel had already seen that it "came up among them" (7:8). Thus, this final king, contemporary with the ten, not only arises *after* the first ten (thus the title, "a little one," 7:8) but finally, through his sudden and spectacular conquests of three of the ten (cf. 7:8, 20), looms "larger in appearance than its associates" (7:20) and thus becomes amazingly "different from the previous ones."

The New Testament does not emphasize the initial phase of the career of the final Antichrist. He appears there as ruler of the entire world (e.g., Matt. 24; 2 Thess. 2; Rev. 11; 13; 17; with John 5:43 and Rev. 6:2 being exceptions), with his "deadly wound" already healed by bodily resuscitation (Rev. 13:3, 12, 14). On the basis of chronological comparison (see comments on 9:27), we may designate 7:24 as the first half of the seventieth "week" of Daniel 9, a three-and-one-half-year period immediately following the removal of the church from the world (Rev. 3:10), during which time God will begin His final program of discipline and indoctrination and preparation of Israel for her official function as witnesses to the true God. Although the nation of Israel is still largely apostate during this earlier period, the two special witnesses of God will be carrying on their great work in Jerusalem (Rev. 11:3-13), even while the "little horn" grows rapidly in power among the ten kings and continues his covenant relationship with Israel (9:27).

7:25. And He will speak out against the Most High. This is now the second half of the seventieth week of Daniel 9, a forty-two month period, which begins with Antichrist's rising from the dead, killing the two witnesses (Rev. 11:7), breaking his covenant with Israel (9:27), setting up (through the false prophet) an image of himself in the Jerusalem Temple to be worshiped by all mankind (Matt. 24:15; 2 Thess. 2:3-4; Rev. 13:11-17), and spewing forth incomparably brilliant blasphemies against the living God. These ultimate blasphemies involve the demand that men worship him and a fallen angel (Satan) who strengthens him (Rev. 13:2, 4-6, 14-15). Through the ages, Satan, "the god of this world," has desperately desired that men, bearing the image of God, should worship him (Matt. 4:9-10; cf. Gen. 3:1-5). This will be his supreme opportunity, but he knows "that he has only a short time" (Rev. 12:12).

And wear down the saints of the Highest One. This theme of the sufferings of Israelite believers during their future time of great tribulation is introduced here (and 7:21) in the book of Daniel for the first time, though it will be emphasized increasingly toward the end of the book (8:24; 9:26; 11:32-35; 12:10). Moses had predicted this in general terms (Lev. 26; Deut. 28). Isaiah had spoken about it as a great purging time (4:3-4), and Jeremiah as "the time of Jacob's distress" (30:7). See also Ezekiel 20, Zechariah 12, and Malachi 3. So devastating will be that final phase of "the day of man" that two-thirds of the nation of Israel will die and, "I will bring the third part through the fire" (Zech. 13:9; cf. Isa. 6:13). Israel's Messiah assured her that "then there will be a great tribulation, such as has not occurred since the beginning of the world until now, nor ever shall" (Matt. 24:21). In fact, unless those days are "cut short," none will survive at all, "but for the sake of the elect those days shall be cut short" (Matt 24:22).

Prophetic Scripture emphasizes the extreme plight of God's

people at the hand of the Antichrist at that time, so that he is actually given authority "to make war with the saints and to overcome them" (Rev. 13:7; cf. Dan. 7:21). Just at the time the forces of evil are ready to destroy Jerusalem, the last stronghold of the saints, "the Lord will go forth and fight against those nations" (Zech. 14:1-3), and the remnant will be rescued. Large numbers of Israelites will already have fled to the wilderness regions (Rev. 12:13-16), as Jesus advised (Matt. 24:15-20), and 144,000 others, sealed by God from death (though not from extreme suffering, Matt. 25:35-40), will carry "this gospel of the kingdom" to "the whole world for a witness to all nations, and then the end shall come" (Matt. 24:14; Rev. 7:1-8.

He will intend to make alterations in times and in law. In context, this seems to refer to divine "time" and "law." Satan will know that his "time" is short (Rev. 12:12), but his human instrument (like Hitler, who planned a one-thousand-year kingdom) will doubtless intend to extend the "time" allotted to him in Scripture (Daniel and Revelation) forever. He will learn, however, that his days will decline "in Thy fury," and he will finish his years "like a sigh" (Ps. 90:9), for only God is "from everlasting to everlasting" (Ps. 90:2).

The "law" he will intend to change will probably be the law of God. One law of God is that "the soul who sins will die" (Ezek. 18:4, 20; Rom. 6:23). The Antichrist, speaking for the "father of lies," will seek to reverse this foundational law of the moral and spiritual universe, just as Satan said to Eve: "You surely shall not die!" (Gen. 3:4). God pronounces "woe to those who call evil good, and good evil; who substitute darkness for light and light for darkness" (Isa. 5:20). He will indeed be "the man of lawlessness" (2 Thess. 2:3) and will culminate the desire of fallen men throughout history to cast off every divine restraint that has been imposed upon the world for man's good (Ps. 2:1-3).

They will be given into his hand for a time, times, and half a time. Since this final period of Israel's testing is said to last for

1,260 days (Rev. 11:3; 12:6), which is forty-two months (Rev. 13:5), three-and-a-half years (half of the seven-year covenant period, Dan. 9:27), "time" must be one year, "times" must be two years, and "half a time" must be half a year—thus, *three-and-one-half years*. The same expression appears in 12:7. (On this basis, it may be assumed that the seven "times" God pronounced upon Nebuchadnezzar were likewise years, 4:16, 25, 32.) The amazing conquests of such militarists as Alexander, Napoleon, and Hitler will all be completely eclipsed by the global dominion of the Antichrist. As God prepared Israel for the brightness of David by the darkness of Saul, so also, on a vastly greater scale, the ultimate hour of darkness of our invisible enemy (John 12:31) will be overwhelmed by "the sun of righteousness" which "will rise with healing in its wings" (Mal. 4:2).

7:26. His dominion will be taken away, annihilated and destroyed forever. The thoroughness of the Antichrist's destruction here parallels the effect of the crushing Stone of Daniel 2 (Zech. 11:17). The New Testament confirms this vision, for "that lawless one" will be slain "with the breath of His mouth" and will be brought "to an end by the appearance of His coming" (2 Thess. 2:8). Furthermore, he and his false prophet will be "thrown alive into the lake of fire which burns with brimstone" (Rev. 19:20), and, together with the "father" of this unholy trio, Satan himself, "they will be tormented day and night forever and ever" (Rev. 20:10).

7:27. Then the sovereignty, the dominion, and the greatness of all the kingdoms under the whole heaven will be given to the people of the saints of the Highest One. This clarification of 7:22 must also be harmonized with the promise that the everlasting kingdom will be given to Christ (7:13-14). The Son of Man graciously shares His dominion with His blood-bought children. The marvelous promise that God gives to His people is that "if we endure, we shall also reign with Him" (2 Tim. 2:12). Isaiah saw the day when the spoils of victory would be divided by the Messiah with His people, called, by His grace, "the great" and "the strong" (Isa. 53:12). In light of this, Paul insisted that "the sufferings of this present time are not worthy to be compared with the glory which is to be revealed to us" (Rom. 8:18). And John tells us that shortly after the destruction of the Antichrist at the second coming of Christ, "I saw thrones, and . . . the souls of those who had been beheaded because of the testimony of Jesus . . . and they came to life and reigned with Christ for a thousand years . . . they will be priests of God and of Christ and will reign with Him for a thousand years" (Rev. 20:4, 6). God's people in the midst of intense suffering for Him will never be disappointed in their hope of reigning with Him, for such hope is God's means of giving us maturity (Rom. 5:3-5).

4. *Conclusion* (7:28)

7:28. As for me, Daniel, my thoughts were greatly alarming me and my face grew pale, but I kept the matter to myself. Just as the vision itself had brought distress and alarm to Daniel (7:15), so also did the interpretation of it by the angel. The emotional shock to this man of God almost overwhelmed him, as he contemplated the cosmic scope of the conflict between good and evil, light and darkness in the spiritual realm. Later visions would have a similar impact (8:27; 10:9); Daniel, like Paul (2 Cor. 1-7), determined not to use such things to attract attention to himself. With Belshazzar now on the throne of Babylon, there was probably no one in the royal court who could appreciate the marvels of God's revelations to Daniel. "Do not give what is holy to dogs," our Lord warned His disciples, "and do not throw your pearls before swine, lest they trample them under their feet, and turn and tear you to pieces" (Matt. 7:6). Though he "kept the matter" to himself, Daniel later recorded this vision for God's people (see comments on 8:26; 12:4).

8

THE RAM, THE MALE GOAT, AND THE LITTLE HORN

III. GOD'S RULE OVER ISRAEL'S FUTURE (Daniel 8-12)

A. DANIEL'S DREAM OF THE RAM, THE MALE GOAT, AND THE LITTLE HORN (8:1-27)

1, *The Ram and the Male Goat (8:1-8)*

8:1 In the third year of the reign of Belshazzar the king. The introduction to the book of Daniel (1:1—2:4) and the final chapters of the book beginning at this verse (8:1—12:13) were written in Hebrew with the people of Israel primarily in perspective. Daniel 2:4—7:28 was written in Aramaic, the common commercial language of the Fertile Crescent, to reach an ever wider audience for the sake of witness to the true God of Israel (see comments at 2:4). It is fascinating that the Aramaic section begins and ends with the two perspectives of the four great Gentile kingdoms (chaps. 2 and 7). Similarly, the book of Jeremiah was written mainly to Israel, but the one verse in the book that aims at the wider audience is written in Aramaic and contains a powerful challenge to the false gods of the Gentile world: "Thus you shall say to them, 'The gods that did not make the heavens and the earth shall perish from the earth and from under the heavens'" (Jer. 10:11).

The year is now 551 B.C., and the situation in the Neo-Babylonian kingdom is ominous. King Nabonidus has departed for Arabia, leaving Babylon in the hands of an unworthy son, Belshazzar (see 5:22-24, and comments on 5:1). Already the collapse of the weakened empire is visibly imminent, for within one year, Cyrus son of Cambyses, a Persian prince, will conquer the great Median empire under the feeble rule of Astyages in Ecbatana and will prepare this dual kingdom for the conquest of Babylon twelve years later (539 B.C.).

A vision appeared to me, Daniel, subsequent to the one which appeared to me previously. Daniel is here referring to the vision of chapter 7, which was given to him by God two years earlier (553 B.C.).

8:2. In the vision . . . I was in the citadel of Susa, which is in the province of Elam . . . beside the Ulai Canal. Just as Ezekiel had been transported in a vision from Babylonia to Jerusalem's Temple (Ezek. 8:1-3; 40:1-5), so now Daniel, in his vision (fully awake now, in contrast to 7:1), finds himself 350 miles east of Babylon in the very birthplace of the Medo-Persian empire, the headquarters of Cyrus. Susa (KJV, "Shushan") had been destroyed by the Assyrians in 645 B.C. and would soon be beautifully rebuilt by Darius I (522-486 B.C.). It was here that the events of the book of Esther took place (483-473 B.C.) and also the early ministry of Nehemiah the cupbearer of Artaxerxes I in the year 446/45 B.C. The Ulai Canal is now the Lower Karun river.[1]

8:3. Behold, a ram which had two horns . . . the two horns were long, but one was longer than the other, with the longer one coming up last. The angel Gabriel later explains to Daniel that the ram (male sheep) "represents the kings of Media and Persia" (8:20). This provides powerful confirmation of the identification of the silver arms of the image (2:32) and the two-sided bear (7:5) as the dual monarchy of Medo-Persia. So now prophetic Scripture rivets our attention onto the *second* of the four empires and reminds us that the "one coming last"

---

1. For further documentation and analysis of the fascinating events that occurred in Susa in the days of Xerxes (483-473 B.C.), see John C. Whitcomb, *Esther: The Triumph of God's Sovereignty* (Chicago: Moody, 1979).

was "longer than the other," thus confirming that Persia, under Cyrus, was the newest element of the dual monarchy and also superseded the Median element as time went on.

8:4. I saw the ram butting westward, northward, and southward . . . he did as he pleased and magnified himself. The three directions of Cyrus's great military movements (and of Cambyses, Darius I, and Xerxes) could refer to the Medes (northward), Croesus of Lydia in Asia Minor and later into Greece (westward), and Babylon and Egypt (southward). Compare the visionary detail of the "three ribs" in the mouth of the two-sided bear (7:5). Cyrus indeed carved out for himself the greatest empire the Near Eastern world had ever known.

8:5. Behold, a male goat was coming from the west over the surface of the whole earth without touching the ground; and the goat had a conspicuous horn between his eyes. Gabriel explained this goat as representing "the kingdom of Greece" (8:21). There can be no doubt, therefore, that the "conspicuous horn between his eyes" was Alexander the Great, for Gabriel explained that "the large horn that is between his eyes is the first king" (8:21; 11:3). Sweeping into Asia Minor with 40,000 men in 334 B.C., he succeeded in conquering the entire Persian Empire, even to the borders of India, in an incredibly short period of time ("without touching the ground") and died at the age of 33 (323 B.C.).

8:6-7. And he came up to the ram . . . and rushed at him in his mighty wrath and . . . hurled him to the ground and trampled on him, and there was none to rescue the ram from his power. Alexander's first victory against the Persians was at the Granicus river near the Hellespont (334 B.C.). After taking all of Asia Minor, he crushed the army of Darius III of Medo-Persia in northern Syria (the Battle of Issus, 333 B.C.). The island fortress of Tyre fell after a remarkable seven-month siege, and in 332 he conquered Egypt without a battle. Acclaimed as a deity, he founded Alexandria and moved on to Mesopotamia where he met Darius III again and defeated him

(Gaugamela, 331 B.C.). Babylon, Susa, Persepolis, and Ecbatana fell before him (330). By now Darius III had been murdered, and Alexander pushed his armies into Bactria and Sogdiana, down through what is modern Afghanistan to the borders of India. There, in his final great victory, he overcame the war elephants of King Porus (Battle of the Jhelum, 326 B.C.) and led his exhausted and discontented troops back to Susa (324 B.C.). Truly, he was one of the greatest military leaders of all time.

8:8. Then the male goat magnified himself exceedingly. But as soon as he was mighty, the large horn was broken. Having carved out an empire of 1.5 million square miles, Alexander provoked many of his Macedonian leaders to rebellion by claiming to be a god, by merging Persian and Greek elements in his army, and by marrying Persian women.

> His mind full of new projects, Alexander built a fleet to explore the coasts of Arabia and Africa. He sailed up the Tigris to Opis, the ancient Assyrian city where Cyrus the Persian had defeated the Babylonians in 539. . . . Alexander entered Babylon for the last time in the spring of 323. Worn out by wounds, hardship and overdrinking, he fell ill of a fever. Soon he could neither move nor speak. He was propped up and each officer and soldier filed past. He acknowledged each man with his eyes or a slight movement of his head. Within two days Alexander died. He was not yet thirty-three years old.[2]

In its place there came up four conspicuous horns toward the four winds of heaven. Great as his military conquests may have been, Alexander failed to create a unified empire. No sooner was he dead than his generals began to quarrel over the government of the empire. They are known as the *Diadochi* ("successors"). The four leading rulers were Antigonus of Babylon and North Syria (soon to be overtaken by Seleucus I Nicator);

2. *Greece and Rome* (Washington, D.C.: National Geographic Society, 1968), p. 246. See also Peter Green, *Alexander the Great* (New York: Praeger, 1970), p. 259; and Mary Renault, *The Nature of Alexander* (New York: Random, Pantheon, 1975), p. 230.

Ptolemy I Soter of Egypt; Cassander of Macedonia; and Lysimachus of Thrace and Bithynia. The same division is described in 11:4 (see comments on 7:6).

2. The Little Horn (8:9-14)

8:9. And out of one of them came forth a rather small horn which grew exceedingly great toward the south, toward the east, and toward the Beautiful Land. Within twenty years, Antigonus had lost Babylon and Syria to Seleucus I Nicator, the first of the "kings of the north" listed in 11:5-35. Over a hundred years still later, out of the Seleucid dynasty, "came forth a rather small horn" by the name of Antiochus IV Epiphanes, the eighth king of this dynasty (175-164 B.C.). He is the "despicable person" of 11:21 and one of the greatest persecutors Israel has ever known. For the possible eschatological significance of this person, compare the discussion on 8:23-25. "The horn, small in the beginning, grows 'exceedingly great' in three directions . . . The implication is that the point of reference is Syria, that 'the south' is equal to Egypt, and 'the east,' in the direction of ancient Medo-Persia or Armenia, and [the Beautiful Land or] 'glorious land' referring to Palestine or Canaan, which lay between Syria and Egypt . . . with the word for 'land' supplied from Daniel 11 (cf. Dan. 11:16, 41, 45; Jer. 3:19; Ezek. 20:6, 15; Mal. 3:12)."[3]

8:10. And it grew up to the host of heaven and caused some of the host and some of the stars to fall to the earth, and it trampled them down. In biblical symbolism "stars" frequently refer to angels (cf. Job 38:7; Rev. 12:4), but in other cases they can mean spiritual leaders (cf. 12:3 and probably in Rev. 2-3). The latter view seems preferable in this context, for Gabriel tells Daniel that this person "will destroy mighty men and the holy people" (8:24). History provides the account of his devastating persecutions of God's people in Judah and Jerusalem especially from 167 to 164 B.C. (see comments on 8:13-14).

---

3. John F. Walvoord, *Daniel: The Key to Prophetic Revelation* (Chicago: Moody, 1971), p. 185.

8:11. It even magnified itself to be equal with the Commander of the host; and it removed the regular sacrifice from Him. The "Commander" of the people of God, in the light of 8:25 ("the Prince of princes") is probably God Himself, rather than the Jewish high priest (who served as the supreme ruler of the Jews during these centuries when there was no king). "The regular sacrifice" (*tāmȋḏ*) means literally "continuousness" but obviously refers to the regular ceremonial observances in the Tabernacle/Temple (cf. Ex. 29:38; Num. 28:3; Dan. 8:12-13; 11:31; 12:11). In shocking contradiction to his name *Epiphanes* (which refers to glorious manifestations that belong only to God), Antiochus IV in 169 B.C. not only "arrogantly entered the sanctuary and took the golden altar," the lampstand for the light, but two years later "sent letters by messengers to Jerusalem . . . to profane Sabbath and feasts, to defile the sanctuary and the priests, to build altars and sacred precincts and shrines for idols, to sacrifice swine and unclean animals," and to "forget the law and change all the ordinances" (1 Macc. 1:41-49). Finally, in December 167 B.C., "they erected a desolating sacrilege upon the altar of burnt offering, . . . and on the 25th day of the month they offered sacrifice on the altar which was upon the altar of burnt offering" (1 Macc. 1:54-59).

And the place of His sanctuary was thrown down. Even though Antiochus did not totally destroy the sanctuary, he so polluted and desecrated it that three years later, after the Syrian armies were driven out, Judas Maccabeus and his courageous compatriots actually "rebuilt the sanctuary and the interior of the temple" and "replaced the altar of burnt offering" (1 Macc. 4:43-48).

8:12. And on account of transgression the host will be given over to the horn along with the regular sacrifice; and it will fling truth to the ground and perform its will and prosper. It is possible that the "transgression" refers to that of "the host" (the people of Israel). But in the light of the use of this term in verse 13, it more probably refers to the transgression committed by Antiochus. Thus, not only will the people of Israel be subjected to him, but also their regular sacrifices will be stopped, and the precious truths of God's revealed Word will be utterly degraded. Thus, "the books of the law which they found they tore in pieces and burned with fire. Where the book of the covenant was found in the possession of anyone, or if anyone adhered to the law, the decree of the king condemned them to death" (1 Macc. 1:56-57). Antiochus (and Satan) knew that the uniqueness of Israel and her sacrificial system depended totally upon the truth and availability of her written laws.

8:13. Then I heard a holy one speaking, and another holy one said to that particular one who was speaking, "How long will the vision about the regular sacrifice apply, while the transgression causes horror, so as to allow both the holy place and the host to be trampled? Daniel then overheard two angels discussing the length of time that would be involved in the horrible desecration of God's holy place and His holy people. Two years earlier an angel had told Daniel that the Great Tribulation under the final Little Horn would last for three-and-a-half years (7:27). The exact duration of the persecutions and sufferings of God's people is not only of tremendous concern to those who must endure it, but is of infinite concern to the God who inflicts it. Although wicked human beings are often the instruments of Satan in such persecutions, we learn from the book of Job that Satan himself is actually an instrument of our God in bringing about such testings for the refinement and purifying of His people.

8:14. And he said to me, "For 2,300 evenings and mornings; then the holy place will be properly restored." Based upon the very strong precedent of Genesis 1, where each of the creation days bears a similar formula ("there was evening and there was morning"), we must understand the 2,300 evenings and mornings to mean 2,300 literal days. Other interpretations, such as the 1,150-day theory, face insuperable obstacles. "Generally, expositors even of differing schools of eschatological interpretation follow the idea that these are twenty-three hundred literal days."[4]

But to what period of history do these 2,300 days refer? According to 1 Maccabees 4:52-59, "the holy place" was "properly restored" on the twenty-fifth day of the ninth month of the year 164 B.C. Working backward 2,300 days from that date, we come to the fall of 170 B.C. Now 1 Maccabees 1:10-21 does not tell us specifically what happened on that day, but it does give us a general picture of the frightening events of that period:

> Antiochus Epiphanes . . . [175 B.C.]. In those days lawless men came forth from Israel, and misled many, saying, "let us go and make a covenant with the Gentiles round about us, for since we separated from them many evils have come upon us." This proposal pleased them, and some of the people eagerly went to the king. He authorized them to observe the ordinances of the Gentiles. So they built a gymnasium in Jerusalem, according to Gentile customs, and removed the marks of circumcision, and abandoned the holy covenant. They joined with the Gentiles and sold themselves to do evil. . . . After subduing Egypt, Antiochus returned in the 143rd year [169 B.C.]. He went up against Israel and came to Jerusalem with a strong force. He arrogantly entered the sanctuary and took the golden altar.

We can see from this portion of the remarkably accurate historical document of 1 Maccabees that the beginning of the 2,300 days of trampling of "the host" (8:13), as well as the holy place, could very easily have occurred in the fall of 170 B.C. It was when the apostate Jews "abandoned the holy covenant" and received official authorization from Antiochus "to observe the ordinances of the Gentiles" that this six-year-and-four-month period of horror began.

3. *The Interpretation of the Vision* (8:15-27)

8:15-16. Standing before me [Daniel] was one who looked like a man. And I heard the voice of a man between the banks of the Ulai, and he called out and said, "Gabriel, give this man an

4. Ibid., p. 189.

understanding of the vision. " From between the banks of the Ulai canal Daniel heard a supernatural voice, apparently from God Himself, speaking to Gabriel and commanding him to enable Daniel to understand this vision. If the basic word for "God" (*'el*) is added to the word for "man" used at the end of verse 15 (*geber*), we have the compound name Gabriel, which means "man of God" or "hero of God." This is the first time an angel is named in Holy Scripture. The only other angel given a name is Michael (see comments on 10:13). Thirteen years later, Gabriel revealed to Daniel the seventy-week plan of God for Israel (9:20-27). More than 500 years later, he appeared in Jerusalem to a priest named Zacharias, announcing that he would have a son named John (the Baptist), introducing himself as one "who stands in the presence of God" (Luke 1:19). And six months after that, he announced to Mary the conception of Jesus, the Son of God (Luke 1:26-38).

8:17. He said to me, "Son of man, understand that the vision pertains to the time of the end." The term "son of man," frequently used of Ezekiel, emphasized his frailty and his inability in himself as a mere human being to grasp the magnitude and the marvel of God's person and of His purposes for Israel and the Gentile nations. But what did Gabriel mean when he said that "the vision pertains to the time of the end"? This expression cannot properly be applied to the career of Antiochus IV Epiphanes. Not only did he die a hundred years before his kingdom came to an end, but also his kingdom was followed by another world empire, namely, Rome. "The time of the end" is actually a technical expression that refers to the events that will accompany the second coming of Christ to destroy the kingdoms of this world and to establish His own everlasting kingdom (see the contextual use of this expression in 11:35 and 11:40).

Over and over again, Gabriel emphasized to Daniel the eschatological focus of this part of the vision. For example (v. 19), he said: "I am going to let you know what will occur at the final period of the indignation, for it pertains to the appointed time of the end." Again (v. 23) he pointed to a king who would arise "in the latter period of their rule, when the transgressors have run their course." Finally, Gabriel commanded Daniel to "keep the vision secret, for it pertains to many days in the future" (8:26).

Thus, the chapter divides into two distinct but related sections. Verses 3-14 describe kings and events of over 2,000 years ago, between the time of Daniel and of the Messiah. Verses 17-26, however, building upon the foundation pattern of the blasphemies and atrocities heaped by Antiochus Epiphanes upon the people of Israel, their sacred institutions, and their God, reach far beyond those dark times to the even worse times that Israel must face at the hand of a brilliant, clever, and far more powerful king who will be "insolent and skilled in intrigue" (8:23).

8:20-22. The ram which you saw with the two horns represents the kings of Media and Persia. And the shaggy goat represents the kingdom of Greece, and the large horn that is between his eyes is the first king. And the broken horn and the four horns that arose in its place represent four kingdoms which will arise from his nation, although not with his power. These words provide an important link between events long since fulfilled and eschatological events centered on a person of enormous iniquity toward which they point. For the tremendous significance of these verses in their clear historical identification of the ram and the male goat, see comments on 8:3-5.

8:23. And in the latter period of their rule, when the transgressors have run their course, a king will arise insolent and skilled in intrigue. Were it not for the fact that this king is clearly placed within an eschatological frame of reference, one might easily identify him with Antiochus Epiphanes. However, upon closer inspection, one might ask whether it would be strictly correct to say that Antiochus came "in the latter period of their rule," that is, of the third kingdom. Actually, the third kingdom continued more than a hundred years beyond his death. Furthermore, is it precisely accurate to say that Antiochus would come "when the transgressors have run their course"? Such statements seem more appropriate for the end of man's day, namely, the end of "the times of the Gentiles" just before the second coming of Christ.

8:24-25. And his power will be mighty, but not by his own power, and he will destroy to an extraordinary degree and prosper and perform his will; he will destroy mighty men and the holy people. And through his shrewdness he will cause deceit to succeed by his influence; and he will magnify himself in his heart, and he will destroy many while they are at ease. He will even oppose the Prince of princes, but he will be broken without human agency. To be sure, some of these descriptive phrases do seem appropriate for Antiochus Epiphanes. However, other statements do not strictly apply to him. For example, the expression "he will even oppose the Prince of princes" seems more descriptive of the knowledgeably blatant opposition to the Lord Jesus Christ that will characterize end-time blasphemers than of Antiochus. Also, the statement that "he will be broken without human agency" seems to describe a supernatural rather than a providential judgment.

The death of Antiochus Epiphanes in 163 B.C. is described by the author of 1 Maccabees 6:8-13 in the following words:

> When the king heard this news [that the Jews had torn down the abomination he had erected upon the altar in Jerusalem], he was astounded and badly shaken. He took to his bed and became sick from grief, because things had not turned out for him as he had planned. He lay there for many days, because deep grief continually gripped him, and he concluded that he was dying. So he called all his friends and said to them, "Sleep departs from my eyes and I am downhearted with worry. I said to myself: 'To what distress I have come! And into what a great flood I am now plunged! For I was kind and beloved in my power.' But now I remember the evils I did in Jerusalem. I seized all her vessels of silver and gold; and I sent to destroy the inhabitants of Judah without good reason. I know that it is because of this that these evils have come upon me; and behold, I am perishing of deep grief in a strange land."

In the light of this record, it would seem more appropriate to interpret the phrase "he will be broken without human agency" as applying to the final Antichrist, who will be destroyed supernaturally at the second coming of Christ (Rev. 19:19-20). Another possibility, worthy of more consideration than it is generally given, is that this refers to the eschatological king of the north, whose supernatural destruction is briefly described in Daniel 11:45.

One major advantage of referring this prophecy to the final king of the north rather than to the Antichrist is that it specifically speaks of a king who will come in the latter period of the *third* kingdom. Antichrist is the little horn of Daniel 7, and thus the final king of the *fourth* world empire. God had previously explained to Daniel that the first three world empires (Babylon, Medo-Persia, and Greece) would lose their dominion, but "an extension of life" would be "granted to them for an appointed period of time" (Dan. 7:12; see comments). Thus, in contrast to the fourth world empire (Rome), which will be suddenly and totally destroyed at the second coming of Christ, each of the first three world empires would extend their influence beyond the termination of their official "dominion." Toward the end of the times of the Gentiles, therefore, we should not be too surprised to find certain aspects of the third kingdom still existing.

In the last half of the seventieth week of Daniel it is true that Antichrist will have absolute control of the Gentile world (Rev. 13). However, his dominion during the first three-and-a-half years will extend only to the ten western kings. At the middle of the seventieth week, Antichrist will not only be threatened but actually conquered and killed by the great king of the north who may be identified with Gog from Magog (Ezek. 38-39). Since Gog will never be a part of the "Roman" empire of Antichrist, it is entirely possible that he will be the eschatological extension of the third kingdom, "in the latter period of their rule, when the transgressors have run their course" (8:23). But of the mighty king of the north, Gog from Magog, it can certainly be said with precise accuracy that "he will even oppose the Prince of princes," and that "he will be broken without human agency" (Ezek. 38:14-16; 22-23).

8:27. Then I, Daniel, was exhausted and sick for days. Then I got up again and carried on the king's business; but I was astounded at the vision, and there was none to explain it. Nothing that Daniel had seen in previous visions could compare to the horrors that were unfolded before him with regard to the destiny of his beloved people Israel. This vision of twenty-three-hundred days of atrocities and sacrilege through one wicked king, only to be followed by an even greater instrument of Satan ("not by his own power," 8:24), who would "destroy mighty men and the holy people" (v. 24), was too much for him to endure. The emotional shock was so great that Daniel "was exhausted and sick for days."

Adding to his frustration was the fact that "there was none to explain." Daniel's experience helps us to understand more clearly what Peter meant when he said that the Old Testament prophets "who prophesied of the grace that would come to you made careful search and inquiry, seeking to know what person or time the Spirit of Christ within them was indicating as He predicted the sufferings of Christ and the glories to follow" (1 Pet. 1:10-11).

9

DANIEL'S PRAYER AND THE PROPHECY OF THE SEVENTY WEEKS

B. DANIEL'S PRAYER AND THE PROPHECY OF THE SEVENTY WEEKS
(9:1-27)

1. *Daniel and the Prophecy of Jeremiah (9:1-2)*

9:1. In the first year of Darius . . . who was made king. As the scene opens in this marvelous portion of God's prophetic Word, we are once again in the reign of Darius the Mede, the king who had reluctantly put Daniel into the lions' den (chap. 6). The events of this chapter probably occurred after that, sometime during the first *official* year of Darius, which would have begun in the spring of 538 B.C. and continued to the spring of 537 B.C. (according to the Nisan system of regnal years in Babylonia).

It is important to note that Darius "was made king" (*homlak*, the passive form of the Hebrew verb is used here), and thus Darius cannot be another name for Cyrus, as some evangelical scholars have claimed.[1] Instead, he was a subordinate of Cyrus the Great (see comments on 5:31 for a discussion of his historical identity).

9:2. I, Daniel, observed in the books the number of the years which was revealed as the word of the Lord to Jeremiah the

---

1. E.g., Donald J. Wiseman, "Some Historical Problems in the Book of Daniel," in Donald J. Wisemen et al., *Notes on Some Problems in the Book of Daniel* (London: Tyndale, 1965), pp. 9-18.

prophet for the completion of the desolations of Jerusalem, namely, seventy years. The fall of Babylon in October 539 B.C. was a great turning point in history, for it marked the collapse of Semitic hegemony in the ancient Near East and the introduction of Aryan leadership, which continued for at least a thousand years.

For biblical history in general, and for Daniel and his nation in particular, it was important for even greater reasons. Cyrus was unwittingly used of God to bring an end to Israel's seventy long years of captivity under Babylon (Isa. 44:26—45:7) and in this sense was actually a "messiah" (Heb. for "anointed," Isa. 45:1) for God's people. These seventy years had been imposed by God upon His nation because of their sinful idolatry and for their willful neglect of His appointed sabbatical years (2 Chron. 36:21).

Back in the year 605 B.C. the prophet Jeremiah had predicted all of this with shocking precision: "And this whole land shall be a desolation and a horror. . . . Then it will be when seventy years are completed I will punish the king of Babylon" (Jer. 25:11-12). Daniel was a lad in his middle teens when that prophecy was uttered in Jerusalem. King Jehoiakim of Judah had utterly despised Jeremiah's prophecies, cutting them to pieces and throwing them into the fire (Jer. 36). But young Daniel must have cherished the words of this great prophet of God. Somehow he had managed to obtain a copy of the scroll of Jeremiah's inspired writings, which he treasured.

Nebuchadnezzar and his successors were now dead and gone, but God's Word through Jeremiah was alive and well (Zech. 1:5-6). The question that deeply perplexed Daniel, now in his mid-eighties, was not *whether* the prophecy would be fulfilled—for he fully accepted the divine authority of prophetic Scripture and a literal interpretation of its words, such as the number "seventy" and the time period "years." His question concerned the precise *method* God would use to accomplish this remarkable prophecy and the precise *day* this would happen (cf. 1 Pet. 1:11, "seeking to know what person or time the Spirit of Christ within them was indicating"). Similarly, our Lord has given rather precise indicators of the time of His second coming to earth (Rev. 6-19) but nevertheless warns the Israelite believers of that future day to be ready for His return at any time (cf. Mark 13:32-37). The general recognition of a "fulness of time," and yet an alertness to the imminence of His coming, is a balance of great importance in prophetic Scripture and spiritual life.

The decree Cyrus the Persian issued in the first official year of his rule over Babylonia (spring 538 to spring 537 B.C., identical to the first year of his subordinate Darius the Mede), as recorded in Ezra 1, was God's response to Daniel's impassioned prayer, as well as a fulfillment of prophecy. In like manner, the second coming of Christ has been precisely determined by God from all eternity (Ps. 2:6; 110:1; Acts 1:7), but the prayers of His people for that great event are incorporated by Him into the accomplishment of it (Matt. 6:10). It may be safely asserted that nothing of significance happens in God's program on earth apart from the persistent and believing prayers of His redeemed ones.

2. Daniel's Prayer of Confession and Intercession (9:3-19)

9:3. So I gave my attention to the Lord God to seek Him by prayer and supplications. This is one of the truly great models for prayer in the Bible. It may even have set the pattern for the great prayers of Ezra (chap. 9) and Nehemiah (chap. 9). Its greatness is not due to eloquence or length. We are not heard in heaven through "much speaking" or through "persuasive words of wisdom," but through a childlike faith-response to God's self-revelation in Scripture as we agree with His evaluation of us (i.e., confession) and lay claim upon His precious promises (Heb. 10:19-22; James 1:6; 1 John 1:9).

It is important to note that Daniel does not begin by thinking of himself or even of his people, Israel: "I gave my attention to the Lord God to seek Him." Many of our prayers are unanswered because we are really talking to ourselves and each other. Only God can answer prayer, and He will do so only on His own terms (James 4:2-3) when He is glorified (John 17:1-5).

With fasting, sackcloth, and ashes. In the Bible, fasting was never a means to gain God's attention or to impress Him (Isa. 58:3-12; Zech. 7:5). It was a practical means of setting aside the time-consuming task of meal preparation in order to concentrate on the Lord Himself. Sackcloth and ashes were simply outward signs of an inward spiritual condition. "All our righteous deeds are like a filthy garment" (Isa. 64:6).

9:4-5. And I prayed to the Lord my God and confessed and said . . . we have sinned, committed iniquity, acted wickedly, and rebelled. The large majority of Daniel's prayer is centered on confession of sin—not just Israel's sin but his own as well. Although no particular sin is recorded in Scripture concerning Daniel, we may be absolutely sure that he, like all members of Adam's fallen race, possessed a sin nature from the moment of conception (Ps. 51:5; Jer. 17:9). What made Daniel one of God's greatest saints was not his sinlessness but his sensitivity to the true depth of his sin. Only the Spirit of God can thus activate the human conscience in the presence of God's infinite holiness. Thus, Daniel was no Pharisee, discerning a speck in another's eye while being utterly blind to the log in his own (Matt. 7:3-5).

God is not pleased when His people indulge in morbid introspection, imagining and even parading before others iniquities that do not really exist. This is a dangerous form of judgmentalism (Matt. 7:1-2). On this level, Paul even refused to judge himself (1 Cor. 4:3-5).

The key to spiritual and God-honoring confession is to have a clear grasp of who God is in all of His infinitely perfect moral attributes of holiness, truth, and love. Not until Job could say, "Now my eye sees Thee," could he "retract and repent in dust and ashes" (Job 42:5-6). And not until Isaiah "saw the Lord sitting on a throne, lofty and exalted," and heard the seraphim calling out, "Holy, Holy, Holy, is the Lord of hosts," could he say, "Woe is me, for I am ruined! Because I am a man of unclean lips, and I live among a people of unclean lips" (Isa. 6:1-5).

9:7. Righteousness belongs to Thee, O Lord. Never is there any
hint in Daniel's prayer that God has failed His people. Job's
complaints against his Lord find no echo here. It is Daniel and
his fellow Israelites who have failed Him utterly. In spite of
Israel's horrible spiritual rebellion, "to the Lord our God
belong compassion and forgiveness" (9:9). God had given
more than adequate warnings to the nation in times past and
was now simply fulfilling "His words" (9:12). In conclusion,
"the Lord our God is righteous with respect to all His deeds
which He has done" (9:14).

The ultimate reason Israel today lacks peace, security, prosperity, and spiritual blessing is because of a lack of these very
ingredients of true worship of the God of their fathers and true
confession of their sins. Only the Holy Spirit can "convict the
world concerning sin, and righteousness, and judgment" (John
16:8). In fact, Israel cannot even say, in faith, "Jesus is Lord,"
except by the Holy Spirit (1 Cor. 12:3).

Someday that will happen. Israel will say, "Blessed is He
who comes in the name of the Lord!" (Matt. 23:39). They will
acknowledge that "He was pierced through for our trans-
gressions, He was crushed for our iniquities" (Isa. 53:5). Then
will "a nation be brought forth all at once" (Isa. 66:8), and
"all Israel will be saved" (Rom. 11:26).

Because they have sinned against greater spiritual light and
privilege, Israel must suffer "double for all her sins" (Isa.
40:2), even as "it shall be more tolerable for the land of Sodom
in the day of judgment" than for the Israelite city of Caper-
naum, which actually saw and heard the incarnate Son of God
(Matt. 11:24). This does not mean that Gentiles are innocent
before God, for "all have sinned and fall short of the glory of
God" (Rom. 3:23), and "there is not a righteous man on earth
who continually does good and who never sins" (Eccles. 7:20).

9:11. Indeed all Israel has transgressed Thy law. Israel did not
consciously lie to God when they said to Moses, "All that the
Lord has spoken we will do, and we will be obedient!" (Ex.
24:3, 7). They were simply blind to the horrible capacities of
their own sin natures. God gave His holy Law to Israel not to

save sinners but rather to function for 1,400 years as a reflecting mirror that "through the commandment sin might become utterly sinful" (Rom. 7:13; cf. Gal. 3:19). The gracious provision by God of a symbolic system of animal sacrifices pointed to the Lamb of God who alone could take away the sin of the world (John 1:29).

9:12. Under the whole heaven there has not been done anything like what was done to Jerusalem. The horrors that finally fell upon Jerusalem, in fulfillment of all the warnings of the prophets from Isaiah and Micah to Jeremiah and Ezekiel, are described for us by Jeremiah in the book of Lamentations.[2] Thirty months (two-and-a-half years) of siege by the Babylonians brought starvation, cannibalism, and total destruction. No other ancient city, so far as we know, experienced such a catastrophe as God heaped upon His beloved wife, Jerusalem (Ezek. 24:16-27). When God told Habakkuk what He was about to do, the prophet was scandalized, until God assured him that the Babylonians would, in turn, be judged by God for their wicked motives in destroying many nations (Hab. 2:5-8).

9:13. All this calamity has come on us; yet we have not sought the favor of the Lord our God by turning from our iniquity and giving attention to Thy truth. In contrast to "the bad figs," Jews who remained in Palestine or fled to Egypt when Jerusalem fell, God graciously called the Jews exiled to Babylonia "good figs" (Jer. 24). It was from this remnant group that God brought back to Jerusalem nearly 50,000 under the leadership of Zerubbabel and Joshua in 537 B.C. (Ezra 1-2). Nevertheless, the vast majority of exiled Jews, especially those who so strongly resisted the ministry of Ezekiel (Ezek. 2:3-7) in Babylonia, never did take advantage of the opportunity to return to Jerusalem. They therefore fell under the self-imposed curse of Psalm 137:4-6 and lost the spiritual privileges of God's

---

2. For a comprehensive analysis of Jerusalem's tragedy in 588-86 B.C., see the exegetical commentary on Lamentations by Walter C. Kaiser, Jr., *A Biblical Approach to Suffering* (Chicago: Moody, 1982).

gracious promise to be "a sanctuary for them a little while in the countries where they had gone" (Ezek. 11:16).

9:16. Let now Thine anger and Thy wrath turn away from Thy city Jerusalem, Thy holy mountain. For the first time in his prayer Daniel makes a request of his God. Instead of rushing into the presence of his Lord with a mouth filled with petitions, requests, and demands, Daniel sets a worthy pattern for all saints: (1) Look to God first, with eyes of faith. "The Lord is in His holy temple. Let all the earth be silent before Him" (Hab. 2:20). "Be silent before the Lord God!" (Zeph. 1:7; 2:13). (2) Then confess sin and unworthiness before Him. (3) Then, and then only, make requests of Him. This is not suggested as a legalistically binding order but as an order of priorities if we truly know Him as He is.

It is of great importance that we recognize what Daniel prayed for—and what he did *not* pray for. He did *not* pray for the spiritual well-being of the church, the Body of Christ. He did *not* pray for the prosperity of the saints of all ages. He *did* pray for "Thy city Jerusalem, Thy holy mountain." He prayed for the restoration of "Thy desolate sanctuary" (9:17) and for a reversal of the "desolations and the city which is called by Thy name" (9:18-19).

This distinction is highly important because God's answer is just as specific as Daniel's prayer. The answer sent by God through Gabriel centers *exclusively* on Jerusalem and Israel, and thus bypasses the entire church age. The present church economy or "stewardship" or "administration" was totally hidden to Daniel (see Rom. 16:25-26; Eph. 3:2-10). The eschatological significance of this will be developed in the comments on 9:24-27.

3. The Angel Gabriel Comes to Daniel (9:20-23)

9:21. While I was still speaking in prayer, then the man Gabriel . . . came to me. The angel Gabriel [Heb., "man of God"], called here "the man" because of his appearance (see Gen. 18:2, 16, 22; 19:1, 5), had appeared to Daniel about thirteen years earlier (see comments on 8:15-16) and had helped him to understand that the vision he had seen "pertains to the time of the end" (8:17).

Only Michael, "the great prince who stands guard over the sons of your people" (12:1) is specifically called an "archangel" in the Bible (Jude 9). But Gabriel seems also to have had enormous authority in God's prophetic program for Israel. It was at the beginning of Daniel's prayer that Gabriel received the divine command to bring the prophetic answer (9:23). If, indeed, he came all the way from the third heaven within that short period of time, our imagination is staggered by the possibilities of angelic movement through possibly trillions of miles within minutes. (The expression "in my extreme weariness" in 9:21 could well be translated "being caused to fly swiftly," thus emphasizing the urgency as well as the speed of Gabriel's ministry of revelation.) Nonglorified man is fantastically limited in the physical universe, even in the so-called space age. By the grace of God, glorified men, in Christ, will someday be higher than angels (1 Cor. 6:3; Heb. 2:5).

Gabriel . . . came to me in my extreme weariness about the time of the evening offering. According to his habit, Daniel had already prayed in the morning and would again pray at night (see comments on 6:10). Now was the time for the main prayer time of the day, between 3:00 and 4:00 P.M. Emotionally drained from the intensity of his intercessory prayer for Israel in a late afternoon hour, he was interrupted by God's special messenger from heaven.

The time indication given here is fascinating in its implications. Daniel describes it as "the time of the evening offering." The term "offering" (Heb., *minḥāh*) refers to a sacrifice on the altar of Jerusalem's Temple (specifically the meal and drink offering) as prescribed in the law of Moses. All such sacrifices had ended fifty years earlier in the destruction of Jerusalem by Nebuchadnezzar's armies. Yet, as far as Daniel was concerned, that afternoon prayer hour was just as precious as it was seventy years earlier when, as a lad in Jerusalem, he had probably "seen the smoke rise from the temple site with its reminder that

God accepts a sinful people on the basis of a sacrifice offered on their behalf."[3] Like other remnant believers in Babylonian exile, he could say, "If I forget you, O Jerusalem, may my right hand forget her skill. May my tongue cleave to the roof of my mouth, if I do not remember you, if I do not exalt Jerusalem above my chief joy" (Ps. 137:5-6). Prayers at the Wailing Wall today are only a shadowy and superstitious perpetuation of the Temple-oriented, but profoundly God-honoring, prayers of Daniel, a regenerate "Israelite indeed" (John 1:47).

9:23. You are highly esteemed; so give heed to the message and gain understanding of the vision. The Hebrew word translated "greatly esteemed" (*ḥᵃmûdôt*) "means more literally 'one desired, counted precious,' with the qualifying 'greatly' being taken from the plural form of the word."[4] One who had so consistently exhibited the grace of God in his life for so many years was now specially privileged not only to hear but also to "give heed to the message and gain understanding of the vision." "One of the most important contributions of the Book of Daniel is its novel insistence on the linking of faith to understanding."[5] Biblical prophetic studies are not an indulgence in idle, existential speculations. They involve careful and devoted attention to exegetical and hermeneutical principles, and the reward to God's people is great indeed. May our God be pleased to raise up more of His servants who are "greatly beloved" in this way.

4. *The Seventy Weeks and the Messiah* (9:24-27)

9:24. Seventy weeks have been decreed for your people and your holy city. In all of Scripture, this is surely one of the

3. John F. Walvoord, *Daniel: The Key to Prophetic Revelation* (Chicago: Moody, 1971), p. 215.
4. Leon J. Wood, *A Commentary on Daniel* (Grand Rapids: Zondervan, 1973), p. 246.
5. Andre Lacocque, *The Book of Daniel,* trans. David Pellauer (Atlanta: John Knox, 1979), p. 191. A formal agreement with this statement is not to be understood as an endorsement of Lacocque's theological perspectives by this author.

most significant prophecies. The very background of the prophecy—Daniel's search through previous prophetic writings, his fervent and effectual prayer, the arrival of Gabriel at God's urgent command—all serve to prepare the reader for a truly spectacular statement of divine purpose for Israel. And we are not disappointed. The Messiah is mentioned twice, including a reference to His untimely death. Then an anti-messiah appears to make a covenant with Israel, only to break it. Chronological references are provided throughout, and then a final period of everlasting righteousness involving the anointing of a most holy place.

The first question that confronts us is *the relative chronology*. What are the seventy "weeks"? When do they begin and end? This is an example of chronology's providing a key for identity. Space does not allow here the detailed discussion these questions deserve,[6] but all lines of evidence seem to point to the following conclusions: (1) The term "week" [Heb., *šābua'*] refers to a unit of seven, in this context *seven years*. Therefore, the prophecy deals with a time span covering 490 years. (2) The seventy years began to count at the year 445 B.C., when King Artaxerxes gave official permission for Nehemiah to rebuild and fortify Jerusalem. (3) When Messiah is cut off, the seventieth week is postponed (from man's perspective) to the end time, still future to our own day, and will be concluded with the second coming of Christ and the destruction of the Antichrist.

It should be noted carefully that the prophecy does not focus on the church but rather on "your people" (Israel) and "your holy city" (Jerusalem). See comments on 9:16. This hermeneutical key unlocks the meaning of large numbers of prophetic Scriptures that have remained obscure during the centuries when Israel and the church have been considered to be essentially the same entity.[7]

---

6. See John C. Whitcomb, "Daniel's Great Seventy-Weeks Prophecy: An Exegetical Insight," *Grace Theological Journal* 2, no. 2 (Fall 1981): 259-63.
7. See, for example, Alva J. McClain, *The Greatness of the Kingdom* (Winona Lake, Ind.: BMH Books, 1959).

To finish the transgression, to make an end of sin, to make atonement for iniquity, to bring in everlasting righteousness, to seal up vision and prophecy, and to anoint the most holy place. Six great divine goals for Israel and the world will have been accomplished by the end of the seventy weeks. These goals are not new in Old Testament prophetic Scripture and are presupposed in New Testament prophecy as well (e.g., Acts 3:19-21; Rom. 11:12, 15, 25-29; Rev. 20:4), for they look to the coming Kingdom age, the thousand-year reign of Christ the Messiah upon the earth (cf. Ps. 2:6-9; Isa. 11:1-10).

The first three goals involve the divine and global control of human rebellion in all its forms, based upon the defeat of Satan at the cross (Rom. 16:20; Heb. 2:14; Rev. 20:1-3). First, all rebels will be eliminated from the nation of Israel (Ezek. 20:34-38; Mal. 3:1-4) and then from all Gentile nations (Matt. 24:37-44; 25:31-46), with the unique result that "the earth will be full of the knowledge of the Lord as the waters cover the sea" (Isa. 11:9). Sin will be suppressed and controlled, but not totally eliminated, for as the Millennium continues and children are born to the regenerate parents who enter it, the "rod of iron" aspect of Messiah's rule will become more evident (Ps. 2:9; Rev. 2:27; 12:5; 19:15). Rare cases of open rebellion will be dealt with suddenly and supernaturally (Isa. 11:3-5; 65:20). Thus, Christ will "finish [literally 'restrain'] the transgression" on planet Earth in answer to the prayers of His people and "bring in everlasting righteousness" to the glory of His Father.

To seal up vision and prophecy. Since Christ, in all His glory, will be present with His people, there will be no further need for visions and prophecies. Similarly, in the postapostolic phase of church history, we have no further need of such ministries, possessing as we do the completed revelation of God in Holy Scripture. During the first half of the seventieth week of Daniel two witnesses will prophesy to Israel in order to launch the 144,000 and others into a global witness for Christ after the rapture of the church (Rev. 11:3-12). But all such prophetic ministries will end forever at our Lord's return to earth.

And to anoint the most holy place. This refers to the Millennial Temple, which Daniel assumes his readers were familiar with on the basis of Joel 3:18, Isaiah 60:7, Jeremiah 33:20-22, Ezekiel 37:26-28, and 40:1—48:35. During the Great Tribulation, the Antichrist will desecrate the reestablished Jerusalem Temple (Matt. 24:15; 2 Thess. 2:4; Rev. 13:15). Then, at His second coming, our Lord will come "into the house by the way of . . . the east" (Ezek. 43:3-4) and will cleanse it of all contamination (Dan. 12:11). In this context, "to anoint" means to officially inaugurate into public ministry. "The most holy place" is literally "the holy of holies," placing emphasis on its symbolic sacredness during the Kingdom age. In the eternal state, there will be no temple at all (Rev. 21:22).

9:25. From the issuing of a decree to restore and rebuild Jerusalem until Messiah the Prince there will be seven weeks and sixty-two weeks; it will be built again, with plaza and moat, even in times of distress. Who is "Messiah the Prince" (Heb. *mashiah nagid*)? The answer is clear: "The only person who fits the description is Jesus (Ps. 110:4; Zech. 6:13; John 4:25)."[8]

It is true that God had prophesied many years earlier that Cyrus would declare of Jerusalem, "She will be built" (Isa. 44:28). But the context of that prophecy indicates that his purpose in having the city rebuilt and repopulated was that the Temple might function again. It was certainly *not* refortified, as this prophecy requires ("with plaza and moat"). The first official decree for refortifying Jerusalem and building its walls was issued by Artaxerxes I in 445 B.C. (Neh. 2:4-8).

From 445 B.C. to Messiah the Prince would be a total of sixty-nine weeks (or units of seven years), that is, 483 years. This would bring us to about A.D. 37, slightly beyond the time of Christ's life on earth.

There is a possibility, however, that Daniel intends these

---

8. Paul D. Feinberg, "An Exegetical and Theological Study of Daniel 9:24-27," in John Feinberg and Paul D. Feinberg, eds., *Tradition and Testament: Essays in Honor of Charles Lee Feinberg* (Chicago: Moody, 1981), p. 201.

prophetic years to be understood as 360-day years, rather than normal years of 365 days, thus bringing us to about 33 A.D. In support of this possibility, 9:27 refers to "the middle of the week," a time period which is described in Revelation 11:2-3, 12:6, and 13:5 as lasting 1,260 days, or 42 months. Since Revelation uses 360-day years for its calculations, it seems reasonable to use the same time units in Daniel.[9]

9:26. Then after the sixty-two weeks the Messiah will be cut off and have nothing. In the light of the previous two verses, this must refer to an event occurring *after* the conclusion of the sixty-ninth seven-year period, that is, after 483 years following the issuing of the decree of Artaxerxes in 445 B.C. As Alva J. McClain and many other students of the book of Daniel have pointed out, the placing of Messiah's death *after* the sixty-ninth week but *before* the seventieth (cf. 9:27) demands a gap of time which, in principle, allows for the entire church age (cf. Isa. 61:2; Luke 4:16-21).[10]

Will be cut off and have nothing. "The word for 'nothing' ('*ayin*) is a noun, meaning literally, 'nothingness.' . . . When Christ was crucified, He did so without apparent friends or honor. He was rejected by men, treated as a criminal, and even forsaken by the Father. In the realm of things attractive and desirable, His portion was equivalent to 'nothingness.' "[11]

And the people of the prince who is to come will destroy the city and the sanctuary. And its end will come with a flood; even to the end there will be war; desolations are determined. Obviously, God's people would never "destroy the city and the

9. See Walvoord, p. 228. Harold W. Hoehner lists the supporting evidence for a prophetic year of 360 days *(Chronological Aspects of the Life of Christ* [Grand Rapids: Zondervan, 1977], pp. 135-38). For exegetical and astronomic limitations of the date of Christ's death, see James L. Boyer, *Chronology of the Crucifixion and the Last Week* (Winona Lake, Ind.: BMH Books, 1976).

10. Alva J. McClain, *Daniel's Prophecy of the Seventy Weeks* (Grand Rapids: Zondervan, 1969), pp. 34-35. See also Robert Duncan Culver, *Daniel and the Latter Days,* rev. ed. (Chicago: Moody, 1977), p. 156.

11. Wood, p. 255.

sanctuary," so "the people" who perpetrate such a deed must be wicked ones, and "the prince who is to come," with whom they are identified, must also be wicked. This prince, an eschatological figure in the light of the following verse, is a "Roman" prince, the Antichrist, previously introduced in 7:8, 20, 24-25. Thus, the people of this prince would also be "Roman," that is, members of the fourth world empire of Daniel.

When does this destruction of Jerusalem and its sanctuary occur? Our Lord stated that "Jerusalem will be trampled underfoot by the Gentiles until the times of the Gentiles be fulfilled" (Luke 21:24), and Revelation 11:2 informs us that during the last half of the seventieth week of Daniel (i.e., the Great Tribulation), the outer court of the Temple (and presumably Jerusalem as well) "has been given to the nations; and they will tread under foot the holy city for forty-two months." The terms "trampled under foot" and "the times of the Gentiles" in Luke 21:24 seem to match the description in Revelation 11:2. "However," Walvoord points out, "there is no complete destruction of Jerusalem at the end of the age, as Zechariah 14:1-3 indicates that the city is in existence although overtaken by war at the very moment that Christ comes back in power and glory. Accordingly, it is probably better to consider all of [Dan. 9:26] fulfilled historically [i.e., A.D. 70 and subsequent desolations throughout the present age]."[12]

9:27. And he will make a firm covenant with the many for one week, but in the middle of the week he will put a stop to sacrifice and grain offering. There is no place in history where such an event can be placed, certainly not at the crucifixion of Christ as some have supposed. Nowhere in the New Testament or in early church history did Christ or anyone else make a seven-year covenant with "the many" in Israel and then terminate it after three-and-a-half years.

This important prophetic statement clearly refers to the same time units as previously described in the end-time activities of the Antichrist ("little horn") of Daniel 7, where "he will intend to make alterations in times and in law; and they [the saints] will be given into his hand for a time, times, and half a time" (7:25). The clarification provided here is that the three-and-one-half years of 7:25 *follow* an initial three-and-one-half-year period at the beginning of which the Antichrist "shall cause a covenant [with the many] to be made strong" (literal translation). Then, for some unexplained reason, "in the middle" of this final seven-year period "he will put a stop to sacrifice [*zebaḥ,* bloody sacrifices] and grain offering [*minḥāh,* non-bloody sacrifices]."

The significance of these words must not be minimized. First, for the Antichrist to cause the Jewish sacrifices to cease, the sacrificial system must have been previously instituted. Thus, part of the strong covenant with "the many" in Israel must be permission to offer sacrifices again "in the temple of God" (2 Thess. 2:4). In light of the current situation in Jerusalem, it would take a very powerful person to obtain and guarantee such access by Israel to the Temple area. It seems possible that the "two witnesses" of Revelation 11:3-6, who have irresistible authority in Jerusalem during the first three-and-one-half years, will also be instrumental in arranging the terms of this covenant with the "little horn," for not until they are killed by him (after he "comes up out of the abyss") is he able to break the covenant and terminate the sacrificial system.

Second, "the middle of the week" not only constitutes the end of the covenant and Temple sacrifice period but also commences a dreadful period described in these terms: *and on the wing of abominations will come one who makes desolate, even until a complete destruction, one that is decreed, is poured out on the one who makes desolate.* "The wing" may refer to the summit or the pinnacle of the Temple, "which has become so desecrated that it no longer can be regarded as the temple of the Lord."[13] These "abominations" (cf. 8:13; 11:31; 12:11) are spoken of by our Lord as yet future to His own day: "When you see the ABOMINATION OF DESOLATION which was spoken of through Daniel the prophet, standing in the holy

13. Edward J. Young, *The Prophecy of Daniel* (Grand Rapids: Eerdmans, 1949), p. 218.

place (let the reader understand), then let those who are in Judea flee to the mountains'' (Matt. 24:15-16).

What is this object of great horror? We read in 1 Maccabees 1:54 that the Seleucids "erected a desolating sacrilege upon the altar of burnt offering." Also, 2 Maccabees 6:2 states that the king commanded the Temple to be called "the temple of Olympian Zeus." Apparently, then, a heathen idol was erected upon the sacred altar in the days of Antiochus Epiphanes. Far worse, however, will be the abomination erected in the future Temple. The False Prophet will not only supervise the installation of an image of the Antichrist in the Temple, but there will be "given to him to give breath to the image of the beast, that the image of the beast might even speak and cause as many as do not worship the image of the beast to be killed" (Rev. 13:15). This will be the ultimate blasphemy, a Satanic masterpiece. Our Lord warned that there would be "great signs and wonders, so as to mislead, if possible, even the elect" (Matt 24:24; cf. 2 Thess. 2:9-12).

Stupendous though this horror will be, God makes perfectly clear to His people through Daniel that *a complete destruction, one that is decreed,* will be *poured out on the one who makes desolate.* Thus, evil in the visible and invisible world is totally under God's control, though the saints may be nearly crushed in the process (see Job 1; Dan. 7:25). Just in time, God will rescue and vindicate those who have trusted in Him (Zech. 14:1-3; Matt. 24:22). "The Lord will slay [that lawless one] with the breath of His mouth . . . by the appearance of His coming" (2 Thess. 2:8), and he, the Antichrist, together with the False Prophet, will be "thrown alive into the lake of fire which burns with brimstone" (Rev. 19:20). This will be the end of the seventy weeks of years and the beginning of the millennial Kingdom age with the characteristics outlined in 9:24. Our God and His Christ will be vindicated before the eyes of all in that day (Ps. 2; 72; 110).

10

DANIEL'S FINAL VISION
OF THE LATTER DAYS

C. DANIEL'S VISION OF THE HEAVENLY MESSENGER AND HIS MESSAGE
(10:1—12:13)

1. *Introduction to the Prophecy* (10:1—11:1)

a. Daniel's Condition (10:1-3)

10:1. In the third year of Cyrus king of Persia a message was revealed to Daniel, who was named Belteshazzar; and the message was true and one of great conflict, but he understood the message. The third official year of Cyrus began in the spring of 536 B.C. Two years had now passed since Gabriel revealed to Daniel the prophecy of the seventy weeks. The remnant of Jews under Zerubbabel and Joshua had now returned to Judea and were laying the foundations of the second Temple (Ezra 3). Daniel (still carrying the name *Belteshazzar* given to him seventy years earlier), now in his eighties, having lived throughout the entire Neo-Babylonian empire (cf. comments on 1:21), was too old to return with the remnant and had important ministries to perform on behalf of that remnant in the Medo-Persian government center in Babylon.

The message was . . . one of great conflict. Daniel had already learned of eschatological conflicts in store for his people (7:21, 25; 8:24-25; 9:27) and of persecutions at the hand of the little horn of the third kingdom even before the time of the end (8:10-14). But now he was to learn of great angelic conflicts involving Israel and the nations and of seemingly endless struggles between kings of the north and south, also involving Israel. In contrast to the visions of chapters 7 and 8, however, he finally *understood the message and had an understanding of the vision.* The basic question in our understanding of the book of Daniel is not whether the prophet himself completely understood what he wrote, but whether God has given us further revelation on the meaning of the book of Daniel in the New Testament (cf. 1 Pet. 1:10-11).[1]

10:2. In those days, I, Daniel, had been mourning for three entire weeks. The Hebrew text specifies these as "weeks of days" (in contrast to the "weeks" of years in the previous chapter). Since twenty-one days ended on the twenty-fourth of Nisan (v. 4), they included the entire Passover season (fourteenth to twenty-first). Doubtless he was aware of the impending conflicts the remnant faced in Judea (Ezra 4) and was praying for them.

b. Daniel's Vision of a Heavenly Being (10:4-9)

10:4. While I was by the bank of the great river, that is, the Tigris. This proves that Daniel did not return to Judea with the remnant and confirms the early date of the book (a Maccabean author of the second century B.C. would surely have brought Daniel to Judea!). Daniel was not at the Tigris (only thirty-five miles from Babylon) in a dream (as in 8:2) but in reality (see 10:7).[2]

---

1. Article 18 of the affirmations and denials issued by the Conference on Hermeneutics (Chicago, November 1982), sponsored by the International Council on Biblical Inerrancy: "WE AFFIRM that the Bible's own interpretation of itself is always correct, never deviating from, but rather elucidating, the single meaning of the inspired text. The single meaning of a prophet's words includes, but is not restricted to, the understanding of those words by the prophet and necessarily involves the intention of God evidenced in the fulfillment of those words. WE DENY that the writers of Scripture always understood the full implications of their own words" (Earl D. Radmacher and Robert D. Preus, eds., *Hermeneutics, Inerrancy, and the Bible: Papers From I.C.B.I., Summit II* [Grand Rapids: Zondervan, 1984], pp. 899-901 [also quoted in *Christianity Today* (17 December 1982): 47]).
2. John F. Walvoord, *Daniel: The Key to Prophetic Revelation* (Chicago: Moody, 1971), pp. 241-42.

10:5-6. I lifted my eyes and looked, and behold, there was a certain man dressed in linen, whose waist was girded with a belt of pure gold of Uphaz. His body also was like beryl, his face had the appearance of lightning, his eyes were like flaming torches, his arms and feet like the gleam of polished bronze, and the sound of his words like the sound of a tumult. Because of problems many have found in identifying the speaker of 10:13 as deity, the heavenly being Daniel saw in 10:5-9 is either understood to be divine, but not the same person as the speaker of 10:10 ff, or else he is seen as the same person but is understood to be a mere angel.

The problem of interpreting 10:13 will have to be carefully faced on its own merits; but it is difficult to accept the view that the heavenly being of 10:5-9 is a mere angel. The resemblance to the description of the glory of the Lord in Ezekiel 1:26-28 and in Revelation 1:12-16 is so undeniably clear that exceedingly powerful theological arguments would have to be provided to overthrow such an identification.[3]

10:7-9. Now I, Daniel, alone saw the vision, while the men who were with me did not see the vision; nevertheless, a great dread fell on them, and they ran away to hide themselves. The men who traveled to Damascus with Saul (Paul) heard "the voice" (sound) of Christ speaking to him (Acts 9:7), but they "did not understand the voice" (Acts 22:9). Also, they "beheld the light, to be sure" (Acts 22:9), but saw no one (Acts 9:7). In other words, while being overwhelmed by the literal presence of God, they could discern neither the identity nor the words of Christ to Saul. When God the Father spoke audibly to His Son, the multitude standing by simply thought "that it had thundered" (John 12:29). In the case of Daniel's companions, we are not told that they saw or heard anything unusual but rather that "a great dread fell on them." Possibly, having heard of

---

3. Young, *Daniel,* p. 225. See also Joyce G. Baldwin, *Daniel: An Introduction and Commentary, Tyndale OT Commentaries* (Downers Grove, Ill.: InterVarsity, 1978), p. 178: "the one who appears to him, though he is described as 'a man,' is more radiant than Gabriel and greater than Michael."

the previous effect upon Daniel of supernatural revelations (cf. 7:28; 8:27), and seeing that he suddenly *retained no strength,* and that his *natural color turned to a deathly pallor,* and watching with horror as he *fell into a deep sleep* with his *face to the ground,* they *ran away to hide themselves.* The "dread," however, may have been supernatural.

c. Daniel's First Strengthening (10:10-17)

10:10-11. Then behold, a hand touched me and set me trembling on my hands and knees. And he said to me, "O Daniel, man of high esteem, understand the words that I am about to tell you and stand upright, for I have now been sent to you." Left totally alone before God, Daniel staggered to his feet in response to the touch of "a hand" from heaven. Two years earlier, Gabriel had told Daniel that he was "highly esteemed" (9:23). Now he is assured once again that God considers him to be a "man of high esteem."

But is this a mere angel, such as Gabriel, speaking to Daniel? Or is it the preincarnate Christ who had just appeared to him in a spectacular theophany (vv. 5-6)? The flow of thought in the passage strongly suggests that the one who now speaks to Daniel is the same one Daniel had just heard ("I heard the sound of his words"—twice in verse 9).

But if this is God's voice, how could He say, "I have now been *sent* to you"? Can God be "sent" to a man? The answer is affirmative if we understand this to be the Son of Man sent by God the Father, even as Daniel had seen Him "coming . . . up to the Ancient of Days and was presented before Him" (7:13). Presumably it was likewise the Son of God who said to Isaiah: "The Lord God has sent Me, and His Spirit" (Isa. 48:16), and, prophetically, "He has sent me to bind up the brokenhearted" (Isa. 61:1). In the New Testament, there are fifty-two references to Christ's being sent to fallen men by the Father.

10:12-13. Then he said to me, "Do not be afraid, Daniel, for from the first day that you set your heart on understanding this and on humbling yourself before your God, your words were heard, and I have come in response to your words. But the prince of the kingdom of Persia was withstanding me for twenty-one days; then behold, Michael, one of the chief princes, came to help me, for I had been left there with the kings of Persia. Gabriel had told Daniel that it was "at the beginning" of his prayer that God commanded him to bring the answer from heaven (9:23). So here, God did not have to wait to hear the entire prayer to send the answer on its way. In fact, "before they call, I will answer and while they are yet speaking, I will hear" (Isa. 65:24). That does not mean that Daniel did not need to pray, however!

The prince of the kingdom of Persia was withstanding me for twenty-one days. These words provide for the interpreter a major challenge that cannot be quickly solved by asserting that the speaker is now a mere angel.

First, this heavenly messenger was so great that he could be *an encouragement and a protection* for Michael, the archangelic prince of Israel (11:1). *Michael*, called here *one of the chief princes* (cf. 10:21; 12:1; Jude 9; Rev. 12:7), is presumably the highest of the righteous angels.

Second, it was obviously God who answered Daniel's prayer. Even if the messenger was not divine, could not God have cleared the way for him to reach Daniel immediately if He had wanted to? To say that Satan's emissaries could withstand God's angelic messenger for three weeks but could not withstand God Himself raises serious questions about God's ultimate authority in the angelic and human realms. Michael, disputing with Satan concerning the body of Moses, defeated him by simply stating: "The Lord rebuke you" (Jude 9). If one is shocked and offended at the thought of a demonic prince of Persia withstanding the Son of God for three weeks, what shall we think of Satan, likewise a mere creature of Christ, withstanding Him for thousands of years, until, at last, during the seventieth week of Daniel, Christ strengthens Michael to cast him down from heaven (where he has been accusing God's people before God day and night) to the earth below (Rev. 12:7-13)?

God, of course, temporarily limits Himself with respect to the forces of evil in the world. Otherwise there would be no evil at all. Instructive in this connection are God's dialogue with Satan in Job 1, Satan's (God-given) power to resist Moses in the court of Pharaoh (Ex. 7:11, 22; 8:7), and our Lord's acknowledgment of the postponement of demonic judgment (Matt. 8:29, "Have You come here to torment us before the time?"). During His incarnation, the temporary authority of Satan as the god of this world was clearly affirmed by Christ (John 12:31; 14:30; 16:11; 2 Cor. 4:4; Eph. 2:2; 6:12; 1 John 4:4; 5:19). Obviously, this satanic authority over the kingdoms of sinful men does not compromise the omnipotence of God. What it does demonstrate is that God has a plan and a program for this world, which includes His sovereign prerogative to say to evil forces: "This hour and the power of darkness are yours" (Luke 22:53).

Michael, one of the chief princes, came to help me. Does the Son of God need the help of angels to accomplish His purposes on earth? In His nonglorified incarnate state, following His temptation by Satan, "angels came and began to minister to Him" (Matt. 4:11). At Gethsemane, He asked: "Do you think that I cannot appeal to My Father, and He will at once put at My disposal more than twelve legions of angels?" (Matt. 26:53). Thus, there have been times when the Son of God has chosen to use the "help" of angels. Michael's "help" in defeating Satan's forces will once again be used during the seventieth week (see Rev. 12:7-9).

For I had been left there with the kings of Persia. The word "had been left" means " 'to be left over, remain.' The word sometimes carries the thought of being left in a position of pre-eminence (as on a field of battle), and it is best so taken here. After the struggle with the demon, Daniel's visitor remained preeminent, as victor. . . . The word 'kings' is in the plural, likely because the place of influence won would continue with future kings of Persia . . . a total period, in fact, of more than two centuries, until Greece would take over world leadership.''[4]

10:14. "Now I have come to give you an understanding of what will happen to your people in the latter days, for the vision pertains to the days yet future." As in 2:28 (see Gen. 49:1), the expression "in the latter days" refers not to exclusively eschatological events (as is the case with "the end time" in 11:35, 40; 12:4, 9) but rather to "the entire future history of Israel as culminating in the climax of the second advent and the establishment of the earthly kingdom."[5]

10:15-17. I turned my face toward the ground and became speechless . . . anguish has come upon me, and I have retained no strength . . . there remains just now no strength in me, nor has any breath been left in me. The devastating effect of the theophany upon the aged Daniel was similar to that which aged John experienced on the isle of Patmos: "And when I saw Him, I fell at His feet as a dead man" (Rev. 1:17). If the full glory of the Son of God had been unveiled to these men, they would have literally died, "for no man can see Me and live!" (Ex. 33:20).

d. Daniel's Second Strengthening (10:18—11:1)

10:19. *"May my lord speak, for you have strengthened me."* By way of spiritual application, no man can hear and respond properly to the Word of God unless and until he has been illumined by the Holy Spirit. Only as one receives "an anointing from the Holy One" can he have "ears to hear," for "His anointing teaches you about all things" (1 John 2:20, 27). It was because Israel lacked spiritual strength that they cried out to Moses: "Speak to us yourself and we will listen; but let not God speak to us, lest we die" (Ex. 20:19).

4. Leon J. Wood, *A Commentary on Daniel* (Grand Rapids: Zondervan, 1973), pp. 273-74.
5. Walvoord, p. 248.

10:20. "I shall now return to fight against the prince of Persia; so I am going forth, and behold, the prince of Greece is about to come." Even though an initial victory had been won against the archangelic demon prince of Persia (see comments on 10:13), the divine/demonic struggle would continue, presumably throughout the two hundred years of Medo-Persian history, down to the time of Alexander the Great, when the demon prince of Greece would be confronted on behalf of Israel. Christ our Lord defeated Satan at His first coming (John 12:31; Heb. 2:14), but in another sense the divine conflict against him still continues (Eph. 6:12-13). "We get a rare glimpse behind the scene of world history. There are spiritual forces at work that are far in excess of what men who disregard revelation would suppose. They struggle behind the struggles that are written on the pages of history."[6]

"The mention of both Persia and Greece also directs our attention to the second and third major empires which are involved in the prophecies of Daniel 11:1-35."[7]

10:21—11:1. "However, I will tell you what is inscribed in the writing of truth. (Yet there is no one who stands firmly with me against these forces except Michael your prince. And in the first year of Darius the Mede, I arose to be an encouragement and a protection for him.)" The following sections of the prophecy (11:2 to the end) are hereby entitled "the writing of truth" (cf. 10:1; 11:2). Daniel needed to know that these "unbelievable" predictions concerning Israel were sovereignly decreed and thus certain. We need to be reminded today that these are genuine prophecies and not pseudographs, written after the events they describe.

God does not depend upon creatures to accomplish His glorious goals, though He condescends to use them. Though "the kings of the earth take their stand . . . against the Lord," His Son, His Anointed, is nevertheless installed as King of all the earth (Ps. 2:2, 6-12). Though vast numbers of powerful

6. H. C. Leupold, *Exposition of Daniel* (Columbus: Wartburg, 1949), pp. 457-58 (quoted in Walvoord, p. 247).
7. Walvoord, p. 250.

angels should rebel against their Creator, they will enter into an "eternal fire which has been prepared" for them (Matt. 25:41). The touching note, *there is no one who stands firmly with me against these forces except Michael your prince,* reminds us of our Lord in the Garden, when "all the disciples left Him and fled" (Matt. 26:56), or Paul in his final dungeon: "Only Luke is with me" (2 Tim. 4:11). Presumably Gabriel and other righteous angels had other assignments or were not really qualified for such high-level combat with satanic princes.

And in the first year of Darius the Mede, I arose to be an encouragement and a protection for him. It was in that great first year of Darius the Mede (the first year of Cyrus) that the decree went forth to Israel to return to her land and to reinstitute her Temple services (2 Chron. 36:22; Ezra 1:1). "Though this had appeared to be the free decision of a polytheistic ruler, Michael had been strengthened, his people had been set free to return to their land, all because God's favour was once again towards them. Spiritual factors proved to be all-important in human history."[8] That same year Daniel offered his great prayer to God, which Gabriel answered with the seventy-weeks prophecy, outlining the timetable of Israel's destiny.

Apparently, then, Michael plays a vital part in God's purposes for Israel. When the theocracy of Israel was first created, Michael may have had a prominent part. We know that "the Law . . . was ordained through angels" (Gal. 3:19) and that Michael protected the dead body of Moses from satanic desecration (Jude 9). "The very loud trumpet sound" at Mount Sinai, which "grew louder and louder" until Moses spoke and God answered him with thunder (Ex. 19:16-19), may have been the trumpet of Michael, newly activated by God after 430 years of Israelite bondage in Egypt. Likewise, when God launches Israel again into her worldwide gospel ministry through the work of the two witnesses in Jerusalem following the rapture of the church (Rev. 11:1-13; Matt. 24:14; Rev. 3:10), it will be announced by "the voice of the archangel, and with the

8. Baldwin, p. 182.

trumpet of God" (1 Thess. 4:16). The only righteous archangel named in Scripture is Michael. Thus, during this age of the church, when "the natural branches" of Israel are broken off from the olive tree (Rom. 11:17-24), we may assume that Michael is relatively inactive with reference to Israel, waiting for that great seventieth week to begin.[9]

2. God's Rule over Israel and the Nations (11:2—12:3)

a. Prophetic Preface: Medo-Persia (11:2-4)

11:2. And now I will tell you the truth. Behold, three more kings are going to arise in Persia. Then a fourth will gain far more riches than all of them; as soon as he becomes strong through his riches, he will arouse the whole empire against the realm of Greece. Once again (see 10:1, 21), to emphasize the divine infallibility of the remarkable and almost unique prophetic details to follow, the Lord assures Daniel that he is about to hear "the truth." It is as if He were saying to Daniel, as He did to His disciples centuries later, "Verily, verily, I say unto you . . ."

Behold, three more kings are going to arise in Persia. Since the prophecy was uttered during the reign of Cyrus (cf. 10:1), the three kings who followed him were doubtless Cambyses (530-522), Gautama or Smerdis (522), and Darius I Hystaspes (521-486). This allows the *fourth* to be Xerxes (486-65), the vastly wealthly monarch featured in the book of Esther (and mentioned in Ezra 4:6), who indeed aroused *the whole empire against the realm of Greece.*

9. For premillennial discussions of Romans 11 and the future of Israel, see Alva J. McClain, *The Greatness of the Kingdom* (Winona Lake, Ind.: BMH Books, 1959), pp. 423, 63; Charles L. Feinberg, *Millennialism: The Two Major Views* (Chicago: Moody, 1980), pp. 236-37; Paul Lee Tan, *The Interpretation of Prophecy* (Winona Lake, Ind.: BMH Books, 1974), pp. 196, 232, 247. For amillennial interpretations, see Anthony A. Hoekema, *The Bible and the Future* (Grand Rapids: Eerdmans, 1979), pp. 141-46, 200; and O. Palmer Robertson, "Is There a Distinctive Future for Ethnic Israel in Romans 11?" in K. S. Kantzer and S. N. Gundry, eds., *Perspectives on Evangelical Theology* (Grand Rapids: Baker, 1979), pp. 209-27.

In his great campaign against Greece from 481 to 479 B.C., with an army of probably 200,000 men and a navy of many hundreds of ships gathered from all over his vast empire, Xerxes desperately sought to avenge the humiliating defeat suffered by his father, Darius I, at the battle of Marathon (490 B.C.). But his army was defeated north of Athens at Plataea (479 B.C.), just after his navy was smashed at Salamis, to the west of Athens. In *The Persian Wars,* the Greek historian Herodotus (485?-425? B.C.) describes the planning sessions for the great invasion (which is also referred to in Esther 1:4 as a series of deliberations lasting 180 days): "Xerxes, being about to take in hand the expedition against Athens, called together an assembly of the noblest Persians, to learn their opinions, and to lay before them his own designs. So, when the men were met, the king spoke thus to them: . . . My intent is to throw a bridge over the Hellespont and march an army through Europe against Greece, that thereby I may obtain vengeance from the Athenians for the wrongs committed by them against the Persians and against my father."[10]

11:3-4. And a mighty king will arise, and he will rule with great authority and do as he pleases. But as soon as he has arisen, his kingdom will be broken up and parceled out toward the four points of the compass . . . for his sovereignty will be uprooted and given to others besides them. The prophecy now leaps over 150 years of Medo-Persian history (compare 8:4-5), with no further discussion of the remaining years of Xerxes or of the reigns of Artaxerxes (464-423 B.C.), Darius II (423-404 B.C.), Artaxerxes II (404-359 B.C.), Artaxerxes III (359-338 B.C.), Arses (338-335 B.C.), and Darius III (335-331 B.C.). The highly selective character of biblical prophecy and history (cf. Rev. 12:5-6; John 21:25) is essential for coming to grips with persons

10. Herodotus *The Persian Wars,* 7:8. For a discussion of this great campaign in the light of the book of Esther, see John C. Whitcomb, *Esther: The Triumph of God's Sovereignty* (Chicago: Moody, 1979), pp. 33-37. For an estimate of the size of Xerxes' army, and a full description of his invasion of Greece, see A. R. Burn, *Persia and the Greeks: The Defense of the West, 546-478 B.C.* (New York: Minerva Press, 1968), pp. 326-29 and context.

and events that are crucial, from God's perspective, in the fur-
therance of His kingdom purposes.

*And a mighty king will arise, and he will rule with great
authority and do as he pleases.* This is Alexander the Great
(334-323 B.C.), the "conspicuous horn" of the male goat in 8:5
who came "from the west over the surface of the whole earth
without touching the ground . . . and rushed at him [the Medo-
Pesian ram] in his mighty wrath . . . and hurled him to the
ground and trampled on him, and there was none to rescue the
ram from his power" (8:5-7).

The introductory section of this final great vision provided
the heavenly perspective on these events. Behind Cyrus,
Darius, Xerxes, and other Medo-Persian kings was a satanic
prince against whom the Son of God waged effective war on
behalf of Israel, with Michael the righteous archangel (10:13).
Then, "behold, the prince of Greece is about to come" (10:2(.
Under God was Satan. Under Satan was the demonic "prin e
of Greece." And under this fallen angel, assigned by Satan to
manipulate the kingdom of Greece against Israel, was a man,
Alexander. The secular historian, of course, is preoccupied
with the earthly scene of kings and battles. But no Elisha is
available or needed today to intercede for him (or for us): "O
Lord, I pray, open his eyes that he may see" (2 Kings 6:17), for
God's written and infallible Word gives us, through the Holy
Spirit, the full cosmic perspective that we so desperately need
to grasp the significance of visible events (cf. Gen. 32:1-2; Job
1; Eph. 6:12; Rev. 12:7-9).

If the earthly kings of Medo-Persia and Greece reflect their
demonic counterparts in the invisible world, so also does Alexander the Great anticipate the final mighty and wicked earthly
ruler, who will be neither a mere king of "the north" or of
"the south" but will, like Alexander, "rule with great authority and do as he pleases" (cf. 11:36-39).

As a transition to the highly complex period of history
following Alexander's death (323 B.C.) down to the notorious
"small horn" of the third kingdom, Antiochus Epiphanes
(175-64 B.C.), we are told simply that *his kingdom will be*

*broken up and parceled out toward the four points of the com-
pass . . . for his sovereignty will be uprooted and given to
others besides them.* Daniel had already learned back in 553
B.C. that the third kingdom (depicted as a leopard) would have
"four heads" (7:6). In 551 B.C., he learned further that this
kingdom (now depicted as a male goat) would have a "conspicuous horn," which would be broken, after which there
would come up "four conspicuous horns toward the four
winds of heaven" (8:5-8). Thus, the "four points of the compass" toward which his kingdom would be parceled out are to
be understood as four literal subdivisions of his great but
fragile empire. As explained in the comments on 7:6, these
divisions were ruled by Seleucus I Nicator, Ptolemy I Soter,
Cassander, and Lysimachus.

b. The Kings of the South versus the Kings of the North
(11:5-20)

This remarkably detailed prophecy of the 150-year struggle
between the various inheritors of Alexander's kingdom con-
centrates on Ptolemy I Soter (323-283 B.C.) and his successors
in Egypt (i.e., the Kings of the South) and Seleucus I Nicator
(312-281) and his successors in Syria (i.e., the Kings of the
North). The north/south designation (from the perspective of
Palestine), rather than mentioning Syria (for example) by
name, "fits the predictive character of the passage," for Daniel
would not have known Syria by that name in his day.[11]

It is perhaps significant that this climactic vision of the book
moves away from symbolic figures to plain words. Even when
God did use the "audio-visual method, the 'audio' always
seems to have priority over the 'visual'."[12] Also, even though
"it is unusual in the Bible for distant history to be foretold so
accurately in such lengthy catalogues and with such minute
details" (well over one hundred prophetic details, all fulfilled),
we do find similar details in prophecies concerning Joseph and
the brothers (Gen. 45:5-8) and in the career of Absalom the son

11. Wood, p. 283.
12. Ronald S. Wallace, *The Lord Is King: The Message of Daniel* (Downers
    Grove, Ill.: InterVarsity, 1979), p. 182.

of David (2 Sam. 12:11; 16:22), in the outworking of which "God makes very little, if any, direct or dramatic intervention in order to give any superhuman twist to affairs."[13] The same can be said for the special work of King Josiah, described 300 years in advance (1 Kings 13:2; cf. 2 Kings 23:15-20) and the career of Cyrus of Persia, outlined 150 years earlier (Isa. 44:28—45:7).

Old Testament predictive prophecy does not indulge in irrelevant minutiae but rather in persons and events that are significant in the outworking of God's purpose for the world through His people Israel, just as biblical history is highly selective (though to many untaught readers it seems to be full of meaningless details) and thus truly "prophetic" in character, bringing rich rewards to those who search out and ponder God's precious words.

A recent and highly readable analysis of Daniel 11 with adequate documentation may be found in Walter K. Price, *In The Final Days.* For the most part, however, "attempts to expound Daniel 11:5-20 have been notoriously tedious. A confounding array of unfamiliar names, dates, battles, and political intrigues challenge every endeavor to relate Daniel's prophecy to its fulfillment in the historical events of the third century B.C."[14]

In Daniel 11:5, Ptolemy I Soter of Egypt is foreseen as the first king of the south, with Seleucus I Nicator, "one of the princes," as the ultimate founder of the Seleucid dynasty in Syria in 312 B.C., and thus the first king of the north. Egypt controlled Palestine during the entire third century B.C., though little is known of Israel's history during this period.

In the thirty-year gap between 11:5 and 11:6 (280-249 B.C.), the reign of Antiochus I Soter is skipped over entirely. Then, in verses 6-9, the tragic marriage of Berenice, daughter of the king

13. Ibid., pp. 186-87.
14. Walter K. Price, *In the Final Days* (Chicago: Moody, 1977), p. 38. See also J. P. Mahaffy, *The Empire of the Ptolemies* (New York: Macmillan, 1895); and Edwyn R. Bevan, *The House of Seleucus,* 2 vols. (London: E. Arnold, 1902). A highly readable account of this entire period of Israel's history may be found in F. F. Bruce, *Israel and the Nations* (Grand Rapids: Eerdmans, 1963), pp. 120-60.

of the south, to the king of the north, is spoken of, with some of its evil consequences (249-240 B.C.).

The following section (vv. 10-19) leads up to the spectacular though tragic career of Antiochus III the Great (222-187 B.C.), including his defeat by Egypt at the Battle of Raphia (217 B.C.); his conquest of Palestine, "the glorious land" (198 B.C.); his catastrophic defeat by the Roman army at the Battle of Magnesia (190 B.C.) with the resulting loss of his claims to Greece and Asia Minor; the imposition of an enormous tribute upon him by Rome and the surrender of his son as a hostage (later Antiochus IV Epiphanes); and his death at Elymais.

Verse 20 speaks of the son of Antiochus III, Seleucus IV Philopater, who sent Heliodorus to rob the Jerusalem Temple of its treasures and was then himself poisoned by Heliodorus.

c. Antiochus Epiphanes—The Despicable Person (11:21-35)

The importance of Antiochus IV Epiphanes (175-64 B.C.) in prophetic Scripture is very great. Though he was a relatively unimportant monarch in the ancient Near East, he gained eternal notoriety through his devastating attack upon the people of God and their religion. Thus he prefigured the final Antichrist.

Seizing the Syrian throne illegally from the son of his murdered brother, Antiochus soon demonstrated his qualification for the nickname "Epimanes" (madman). His life-style shocked his contemporaries, but his initial military campaigns were successful. His ultimate goal was to hellenize his empire thoroughly in order to unify it against Rome. Only Judea resisted him in this, though some Jews acted "wickedly toward the covenant" (11:32) and even murdered the high priest Onias III, "the prince of the covenant" (11:22; see comments on 8:9-14). After a successful invasion of Egypt in 169 B.C., he plundered the Temple in Jerusalem and carried the spoils off to Antioch (11:28).

But it was his second invasion of Egypt (168 B.C.) that brought him into deep frustration and Jerusalem to extreme anguish. When his army reached the Egyptian town of Eleusis near Alexandria, he was met by the Roman general, Gaius Popillius Laenas, who demanded that he abandon his Egyptian campaign (11:29-30). Rumors spread in Jerusalem that he was killed. Therefore, he vented his rage upon the holy city, slaughtering and enslaving as many as 80,000 Jews.[15]

The ultimate disaster for Israel, however, involved a systematic desecration of the Temple, including the erection of "the abomination of desolation" (11:31), probably a statue of the Olympian Zeus with the features of Antiochus.[16] Torah scrolls were destroyed, the Sabbath and circumcision forbidden, swine's flesh forced upon the population, and the official sacrifices abolished. Some historians believe this was the first time in history that religious martyrdom occurred.[17]

But even as the final wrath of Satan through his Antichrist will be limited "for the sake of the elect" (Mark 13:20), so now "they will be granted a little help" (11:34). This is clearly a reference to the Maccabean revolt led by the elderly Mattathias and carried on by his son Judas Maccabaeus and other sons, which eventuated in the spectacular cleansing of the Temple in 165 B.C. Ever since then the Jews celebrate the event at Hanukkah ("Feast of Dedication"). One rabbi explains: "On Purim [cf. the book of Esther] we celebrate the annulment of the royal edict to destroy the body; but on Hanukkah we were rescued from the decree which would have destroyed our souls."[18]

The Maccabean revolt, however, was basically a twofold tragedy. First, it quickly sank into carnality and cruelty. This was inevitable because some of its later leaders, such as John Hyrcanus, 134-104 B.C., and Alexander Jannaeus, 102-75 B.C., were notoriously wicked men. God ominously predicted that "many will join them [i.e., the early Maccabean leaders] in hypocrisy" (11:34). Second, they lacked the supernatural presence of the Messiah or even a divinely commissioned prophet to provide the direction and discipline apart from which even a Judean government could not long survive in Satan's world. Note the contrast here with Isaiah 11:1-5, 11-16.

15. Price, p. 116.
16. Ibid., p. 138.
17. Ibid., pp. 139-40.
18. Ibid., p. 157.

Thus, the Maccabean revolt, spectacular in its early years for dedication to the God of Israel, even unto death, soon lost those essential qualities and fell into the hands of the Romans by 65 B.C. It was obviously not God's time for the establishment of His glorious kingdom from heaven.

Verse 35 provides the transition from Maccabean times down through the times of the Gentiles until "the end times." The outlook is one of spiritual blessing ("make them pure") for those "who have insight" even in the midst of great physical trials ("fall," "refine," "purge"). God makes no mistakes with His people. Nothing is left to chance, "because it is still to come at the appointed time." And thus the Lord of all history and destiny lifts Daniel's eyes to see the coming centuries (omitting the age of the church entirely) down to the seventieth week, which is introduced next in terms of the Antichrist and his global dominion.

> The message of the chapter stands out clearly: history as it moves toward its end can be seen to have no clear meaning. Nor will it ever be seen to have any purpose or meaning till we are able to look back on it from the standpoint of what has happened at its end and climax. . . . Where Ecclesiastes proclaimed the nonsense of life without faith, Daniel helps us to see the nonsense of trying to have faith unless at the same time we have hope in what is going to be *at the time of the end.*[19]

d. The Willful King—The Antichrist (11:36-39)

The fact that these events will occur during the future Great Tribulation is suggested by (1) the chronological reference of 12:1 ("now at that time"), which places the events of 11:36-45 into the time of final resurrection and judgment (12:2); (2) the transitional events of 11:35-36, which continue "until the end time"; (3) the broad scope of 10:14, which would fail if its only possible fulfillment, namely, 11:36—12:3, is not eschatological; and (4) what we know of the career of Antiochus Epiph-

---

19. Wallace, pp. 188-89.

anes, which simply does not fit the wording of 11:36—12:1.[20]

Over 1,500 years ago, Jerome (A.D.347-420) explained that whereas Porphyry (A.D. 233-304) and others who denied the possibility of prophetic truth insisted that the final verses of Daniel 11 speak of none other than Antiochus Epiphanes, "those of our persuasion believe all these things are spoken prophetically of the Antichrist who is to arise at the end time. . . . Antiochus is to be regarded as a type of the Antichrist, and those things which happened to him in a preliminary way are to be completely fulfilled in the case of the Antichrist." Speaking specifically of Daniel 11:36, Jerome stated: "The Jews believe that this passage has reference to the Antichrist. . . . We too understand this to refer to the Antichrist."[21]

11:36. Then the king will do as he pleases, and he will exalt and magnify himself above every god, and will speak monstrous things against the God of gods. In contrast to Antiochus Epiphanes, who was a relatively minor "King of the North," this king will attempt to control both the bodies and the souls of all human beings on earth. Satanic pride and blasphemy, shockingly present in Antiochus, will reach their ultimate expression in this "willful king" (from KJV, "the king shall do according to his will"). He is surely the final Antichrist of 1 John 2:18*a* and 4:3, because "the beast" that dominates the central section of John's final book (Rev. 11-13; 17) not only fits the description of Daniel 11:36-39 but also the picture of the "little horn" of Daniel 7:25 (including the chronological framework). From this point in Daniel's final vision to the ultimate and incomparable "time of distress" (12:1), this Roman "beast out of the sea" comes into focus either explicitly (11:36-39) or implicitly (11:40, 44-45; 12:1). What Antiochus Epiphanes foreshadowed, he embodies.

20. George M. Harton, "An Interpretation of Daniel 11:36-45," *Grace Theological Journal* 4, no. 2 (Fall 1983): 208-9.
21. Gleason L. Archer, Jr., trans., *Jerome's Commentary on Daniel* (Grand Rapids: Baker, 1958), pp. 129, 136.

*And he will prosper until the indignation is finished, for that
which is decreed will be done.* The shocking challenge to God's
sovereignty that men will see in this depraved world ruler calls
for clear reminders that evil is not only temporarily tolerated
by God but is actually included in His decree (cf. Gen. 45:5, 7;
50:20). Two years earlier, Daniel had been told in similar terms
that God would accomplish His purposes through this wicked
one "even until a complete destruction, one that is decreed, is
poured out on the one who makes desolate." Thus, a recurring
theme of the book of Daniel is the absolute sovereignty of God
in the midst of human and angelic rebellion (cf. Dan. 4:17, 25).

*11:37. And he will show no regard for the gods [God] of his
fathers.* Will the Antichrist be a Jew? In Revelation 13:1 he is
described as "a beast coming up out of the sea," which symbolizes the Gentile world (cf. Dan. 7:2-3; Rev. 17:15). But he
could be a Jew born and raised in a Gentile nation and still fit
this description. An even more important question is how
apostate Israel will view this person. If they see him as their
Messiah, they would more likely accept him as such if he were a
Jew (Deut. 18:15, 18; 2 Sam. 7:12). But it is not altogether clear
that they will see him as their true Messiah at the time of entering into the seven-year covenant (Dan. 9:27), unless our Lord
implied this in John 5:43 (cf. Matt. 24:5). A key question is
whether *'elohîm* at the beginning of this verse is to be understood as singular ("God") or plural ("gods"), for "the God of
his fathers" would indicate that he is a Jew. The Hebrew wording in the following verse (lit., "in his place") suggests a singular antecedent. Edward J. Young concludes: "The phrase
has a Jewish emphasis and has reference to the Jewish religion.
The one who has no regard for this Jewish religion is himself a
Jew, the Antichrist. I fully agree with Gaebelein's statement,
'Here his Jewish descent becomes evident.' "[22]

---

22. Young, p. 249. Leon Wood, however, denies that "the god of his
    fathers" can refer to the God of Israel, for "the plurality of the word
    'gods' (*'elohîm*) is here used, which is truly indicative of plurality in this
    instance, since the singular form *'eloah* is used twice in the next few
    words" (p. 306).

Or for the desire of women. "he shall set himself free ... from all piety toward men and God, from all the tender affections of the love of men and of God. The 'love of women' [cf. 2 Sam. 1:26] is named as an example ... of that affection of human love and attachment for which even the most selfish and most savage of men feel some sensibility."[23]

11:38-39. He will honor a god of fortresses ... he will give great honor to those who acknowledge him. The Antichrist will lavish all his vast resources upon military fortifications and programs and will encourage cooperation by distributing positions of authority and valuable property to his followers.

e. The Mid-Tribulation Crisis (11:40-45)

11:40. And at the end time the king of the South will collide with him, and the king of the North will storm against him ... and he will enter countries, overflow them, and pass through. "At the end time" is a clear eschatological reference in the book of Daniel (cf. 11:35; 12:4, 9). The king of the south must therefore be a yet future Egyptian monarch, judging from the previous use of the term in this chapter and also the clear statements of 11:42-43. Presumably in alliance with a king of the north (such as Russia today?), the eschatological Egyptian ruler will launch a diversionary thrust and "will collide with him," that is, with "the king [who] will do as he pleases" (the Antichrist) in the immediately preceding context (11:36-39).

It is important to note that the antecedent of "him" (used twice in this verse) must be the Antichrist, whose location at this time will be somewhere between the "north" and the "south," presumably Palestine.

Could the king of the north be Syria? No, for his "attack on Antichrist involves the King of the North's entering, overflowing, and passing through other countries en route to Pal-

23. C. F. Keil, *Biblical Commentary on the Book of Daniel* (1872; reprint, Grand Rapids: Eerdmans, 1955), p. 465. For a discussion of other possible interpretations of this difficult expression, see Walvoord, pp. 274-75.

estine."[24] The name of any particular "King of the North" may indeed change with the flux of history, but the general location remains fixed. "Russia meets the hermeneutical requirements involved in the title 'King of the North' associated with the Seleucid empire [of vv. 5-29]. It has a corresponding northern location, a corresponding vast geographical scope, and a corresponding vast political preeminence."[25]

Although agreeing that three distinct kings are seen in Daniel 11:40-45, most premillennialists understand the pronoun *he* in these verses to refer to the Antichrist, not the king of the north. Thus, when the king of the north storms against him with chariots, horsemen, and many ships, the Antichrist is viewed as launching a counterattack whereby "he will enter countries." This great conflict is seen as continuing throughout the last half of the seventieth week until the Antichrist comes to supernatural judgment at Armageddon.[26]

Among the difficulties with this view are: (1) Rev. 13:4 seems to contradict the idea that the Antichrist will require forty-two months to subdue his enemies; (2) the "rumors" he hears are from Palestine ("the Beautiful Land"), east and north of Libya and Ethiopia, not from the Euphrates River as generally understood (cf. Rev. 16:12); (3) if the king in 11:45 were the Antichrist, 12:1 would seem to be anticlimactic, whereas the Antichrist is the climax of all evil forces until the Second Coming of Christ; (4) it is not primarily Israel, but rather the Antichrist who is attacked by both the king of the south and the king of the north in this passage.[27]

How does the Antichrist finally attain global authority? The clue comes from Revelation 13 and 17: "his fatal wound was healed" (13:3, 12, 14; cf. 17:8, 11). This thrice-repeated statement may presuppose an interpretation of Daniel 11:40-45 that sees the Antichrist ("the king who does as he pleases," 11:36-39) killed by the irresistible king of the north, sweeping

24. Harton, p. 214.
25. Ibid.
26. Ibid., p. 216. For an exposition of the majority view among premillennial scholars, see J. Dwight Pentecost, *Things to Come* (Grand Rapids: Zondervan, 1958), p. 356.
27. Ibid., p. 220.

through countries in his southward thrust into "the Beautiful Land."

The entire passage (Daniel 11:40-45) describing the king of the north thus constitutes a parenthetical background explanation of the stupendous rise of the Antichrist to world supremacy after both the king of the north and the king of the south are removed as threats to his demonic and blasphemous ambitions (cf. Gen. 11:1-9 as a similar parenthetical flashback into Gen. 10). The invasion of Palestine by the king of the north probably occurs only a few months before the events of Revelation 13 (and Dan. 11:36-39; 12:1) and provides the background for them.

The king of the North will storm against him with chariots, with horsemen, and with many ships. Note the threefold emphasis on irresistible military power, and compare with Ezekiel 38:9 ("you will come like a storm . . . like a cloud covering the land [of Israel]").

11:41. He will also enter the Beautiful Land, and many countries will fall; but these will be rescued out of his hand: Edom, Moab and the foremost of the sons of Ammon. Entering Palestine from the far north (passing through "countries" to get there), the king of the north rushes southward into Africa so rapidly that he doesn't even take time to conquer the trans-Jordan areas of Edom, Moab, and Ammon (see Isa. 11:14 for Israel's ultimate conquest of these territories).

11:42. Then he will stretch out his hand against other countries, and the land of Egypt will not escape. The king of the north apparently has no great concern for possible flank attacks on his extended lines of communication with his now far-distant homeland, for the Antichrist has presumably been killed with the sword of the king of the north (cf. 11:40, "he will . . . overflow them, and pass through"; Rev. 13:14). Totally ignoring the alliance with the king of the south, which presumably served as the mechanism for a great pincer attack on the Antichrist, the king of the north now conquers his former ally!

One does not need to look far for contemporary examples of such international treachery.

11:43. But he will gain control over the hidden treasures of gold and silver, and over all the precious things of Egypt; and Libyans and Ethiopians will follow at his heels. In that day, as to some extent today, Egypt (king of the south) may be allied with oil-rich Arab nations and thus, in spite of the presence of an impoverished lower class, will be irresistibly attractive to the king of the north (cf. Ezek. 38:13 for Gog's grasp after silver and gold).

Having destroyed the king of the south and occupying his Egyptian domain, the king of the north now sends his victorious armies westward into Libya and further southward into Ethiopia. Compare Ezekiel 38:5. With all of northeast Africa within his grasp, he seems to be on his way to achieving world dominion. But then, a totally unexpected and electrifying event occurs that eventuates in his complete destruction.

11:44-45. But rumors from the East and from the North will disturb him, and he will go forth with great wrath to destroy and annihilate many. And he will pitch the tents of his royal pavilion between the seas and the beautiful Holy Mountain; yet he will come to his end, and no one will help him. Many have understood "the East" to refer to "the kings of the east" coming to the battle of Armageddon (Rev. 16:12). But the battle of Armageddon occurs at the end of the seventieth week, and these events occur just before the middle of the seven-year period (cf. Dan. 12:1). Further more, the fact that "the East" and "the North" point to Palestine as seen from Africa is confirmed by the movement of the king of the north back to "the beautiful Holy Mountain" (i.e., Jerusalem) rather than to regions to the east of Palestine.

But what are these "rumors" that "disturb" him to such an extent that he abandons his entire African campaign and is compelled to "go forth with great wrath to destroy and annihilate many" and to spread out his vast army "between the seas [the Dead Sea and the Mediterranean] and the beautiful Holy Mountain"?

Various prophetic indicators (e.g., Dan. 9:27; Matt. 24:15; 2 Thess. 2:3-4; Rev. 11:13, 17) focus our attention upon an event of almost cosmic significance that God directs Satan to accomplish in Jerusalem at the mid-point of the seventieth week, three-and-one-half years before the second coming of Christ: (1) The Antichrist receives "the wound of the sword," which kills him (Rev. 13:14; cf. 13:3, 12); (2) he thus enters into the realm of the dead and "is not" (Rev. 17:8, 11); (3) he then is enabled "to come up out of the abyss" (Rev. 11:7; 17:8) to begin a second earthly, nonglorified life as the eighth and greatest enemy of Israel (having previously been the seventh, Rev. 17:10-11); (4) he immediately kills God's two witnesses (Rev. 11:7), suggesting that his death and return to life occur in Jerusalem; (5) the false prophet then erects an image of the Antichrist (Matt. 24:15, "the ABOMINATION OF DESOLATION ... standing in the holy place"), is enabled to give it the breath of life and the power to kill all opponents (Rev. 13:14-15), insists that the Antichrist is God Almighty (2 Thess. 2:4), and brings down fire from heaven to demonstrate it (Rev. 13:13); (6) the Antichrist breaks his seven-year covenant with Israel (Dan. 9:27) and begins a forty-two month persecution of the believing remnant of Israel (Rev. 12:6, "the woman fled into the wilderness ... one thousand two hundred and sixty days").

The detailed scenario of prophetic events surrounding the beginning of the final phase of the Antichrist's career on earth points back to and presupposes the destruction of his ultimate earthly enemy. This enemy is not described in the New Testament because ample information is provided in Daniel 11:40-45, which in turn builds upon Ezekiel 38-39 (Gog from Magog).

But even Gog was not a new figure in Old Testament prophecy: "Thus says the Lord God, 'Are you the one of whom I spoke in former days through My servants the prophets of Israel, who prophesied in those days for many years that I would bring you against them?'" (Ezek. 38:17). Looking farther back along the line of progressive revelation, we find Joel speaking of the fate of a great "northern army," which will do "great things" and yet will be destroyed between Palestine's "eastern sea" and "western sea" (Joel 2:20). Isaiah and Micah, in the late eighth century B.C., saw this one as "the Assyrian," using the name of a familiar northern military power as a contemporary analogy for the final "king of the north" (Isa. 10:12, 24-27; Micah 5:5-6).[28]

Now where are the connections between the Old Testament prophetic picture of the destruction of the great king of the north and the rise of the Antichrist who will overcome the saints (Dan. 7:21; Rev. 13:7) and gain control of the entire earth (Rev. 13:7, 8)?

One clear connection is the destruction of the king of the north (i.e., Gog) by fire from heaven, as described by Ezekiel: "I shall rain on him, and on his troops . . . a torrential rain, with hailstones, fire, and brimstone . . . on the mountains of Israel" (Ezek. 38:22; 39:4). This supernatural destruction by fire (cf. Ex. 9:23-24) will either be indirectly delegated by God to Satan (cf. Job 1:12, 16) or will be accomplished directly. In either case, the false prophet performs a similar miracle (Rev. 13:13), perhaps claiming that he, through Satan, had thus destroyed the great northern army in the land of Israel, leaving the Beast/Antichrist in full control of the world.

Another close connection between the Old Testament and the New Testament in this crucial event is the return of the Roman "Beast" from the realm of the dead. It will be on this basis that "the whole earth" will be "amazed," will "follow after the beast" (Rev. 13:3), and will ask, "Who is like the beast, and who is able to wage war with him?" (Rev. 13:4). It seems rather obvious that the Beast/Antichrist is killed by some great king in a battle (Rev. 13:14, "the wound of the sword"), comes back to life (Rev. 13:3, 12, 14), and then

28. See William F. Foster, "The Eschatological Significance of the Assyrian in the Old Testament," Th.D. diss. (Grace Theological Seminary, 1956). For the view that Ezekiel 38-39 refers to the brief period at the end of the Millennium, see Ralph H. Alexander, "A Fresh Look at Ezekiel 38 and 39," *Journal of the Evangelical Theological Society* 17, no. 3 (Summer 1974): 157-69.

somehow destroys (or at least claims to have destroyed) his mighty enemy so that all mankind trembles before him. What great enemy could this be, if it is not the "northern army" of Joel, the eschatological Assyrian of Isaiah and Micah, and the Gog of Ezekiel? This is the king of the north in Daniel 11:40-45, who defeats the willful king of Daniel 11:36-39 and who, in turn, mysteriously "will come to his end" so that "no one will help him" just before Israel enters into "a time of distress such as never occurred since there was a nation until that time" (Dan. 12:1).

Thus the great king of the north passes off the scene by the midpoint of the seventieth week and serves New Testament eschatology only as a necessary backdrop or launching pad for the Antichrist, the ultimate masterpiece of Satan. The king of the north will be the inflictor of the "fatal wound" upon this Beast and thus will prove to be the greatest military challenge on earth for the false christ who gallops forth in the beginning of the seventieth week, "conquering and to conquer" (Rev. 6:2). By carefully comparing Scripture with Scripture, Old Testament with New Testament, this highly complex phase of end-time events gradually takes shape in the mind's eye of the student of God's prophetic Word.

f. The Final Deliverance of Israel (12:1-3)

12:1. Now at that time Michael, the great prince who stands guard over the sons of your people, will arise. If the events of 11:40-45 reach their climax at the middle of the seventieth week, we would expect Michael to "arise" also "at that time." This seems to be confirmed by Revelation 12:7-12, which dates the final victory of Michael over Satan 1,260 days (12:6), or three-and-one-half "times" (12:14), before the second coming of Christ. If Israel needed Michael's help in the days of Daniel (cf. comments on Dan. 10:13, 21), she shall need it even more in her final great tribulation.

And there will be a time of distress such as never occurred since there was a nation until that time. Previous revelation (e.g., Dan. 7:21, 25; 8:23-25; 9:27) and later revelation (e.g., Zech.

11:15-17; Matt. 24:15-24; 2 Thess. 2:3-4; Rev. 13) emphasize not only the time period of special distress for Israel that is coming but also the horrible visible instrument of that distress, the Antichrist. Thus, the willful king of Daniel 11:36-39, the final victor against the king of the north in 11:45, becomes the ultimate persecutor of Michael's people, Israel.[29]

And at that time your people, everyone who is found written in the book, will be rescued. "While 12:1b-3 does not *say* that this is the work of Messiah, later revelation also makes it plain that it will be the Christ who rescues Israel (12:1), who will resurrect the dead (12:2), and who will reward the righteous (12:3). Consequently, this brings the argument of the book to a climax. The Gentile nations dominating Israel, beginning with Babylon, would not soon end. Persia, Greece, and Rome would follow. But at the appointed time in history's darkest hour, Messiah will come and reign forever. God rules."[30]

Christ will rescue His people "at that time" through various means at His disposal. The two witnesses whom Antichrist kills will be resurrected and will visibly ascend to heaven (Rev. 11:11-12); their 144,000 disciples will be sealed (Rev. 7:3-8); the bulk of the nation will be "nourished" 1,260 days (Rev. 12:6), whereas Satan's pursuing armies are swallowed up by the earth (12:15-16); those few believers who physically survive the Great Tribulation will be honored (Matt. 25:31-40); and those beheaded for their testimony will be raised from the dead to reign with Him (Rev. 20:4).

12:2. And many of those who sleep in the dust of the ground will awake, these to everlasting life, but others to disgrace and everlasting contempt. In this context, "awake" refers to bodily (not spiritual) resurrection (cf. Job 14:12; Ps. 17:15; 1 Thess. 5:10), for unbelievers will have the same experience. However, it is important to note that not *all* "of those who sleep in the dust of the ground" will "awake" *at that time.* It will not be a general resurrection of all who have died throughout history.

29. Harton, p. 230.
30. Ibid., p. 231.

In the progress of revelation, the apostle Paul makes clear in 1 Corinthians 15:23-24 the chronological sequence (Gk., *tagma*) of all resurrections: "Christ the first fruits, after that [over 1,900 years now] those who are Christ's at His coming, then comes the end [the second resurrection, that of unbelievers, 1,000 years later; Rev. 20:5-6]." Thus, a valid paraphrase of the verse would be: "And many from among the sleepers of the dust of the earth shall awake; these shall be unto everlasting life; but those, the rest of the sleepers, those who do not awake at this time, shall be unto shame and everlasting contempt."[31]

To everlasting life. This is the first mention of this expression in the Old Testament, and it carries the same meaning in the New Testament.

12:3. And those who have insight will shine brightly like the brightness of the expanse of heaven, and those who lead the many to righteousness, like the stars forever and ever. "Those who have insight" (same expression as in 11:33, 35) are like those in the days of Antiochus Epiphanes who demonstrated their willingness to die for God's eternal truth. The "insight" here is obviously spiritual wisdom, primarily because of the recorded effect. Such wisdom is desperately needed in our churches today, and especially in centers where church leaders are being trained.

And those who lead the many to righteousness, like the stars forever and ever. The "many" who are led to righteousness refers back to the "many" of verse 2, thus confirming that the latter are believers only.[32] Our Lord may have been alluding to Daniel's prophecy of those who "will shine brightly . . . like the stars" when he said that at the end of this age "the

31. Samuel P. Tregelles, *Remarks on the Prophetic Visions in the Book of Daniel,* 7th ed. (London: The Sovereign Grace Advent Testimony, 1965), p. 164 (cited and discussed by Robert D. Culver, *Daniel and the Latter Days,* rev. ed. [Chicago: Moody, 1977], p. 186).

32. Wood, p. 319.

righteous will shine forth as the sun in the kingdom of their Father." Then he added, "He who has ears, let him hear" (Matt. 13:43).

3. *Final Instructions and Questions* (12:4-13)

a. Preserving the Written Revelation (12:4)

12:4. But as for you, Daniel, conceal these words and seal up the book until the end of times. The same word translated here "conceal" appears in 8:26 ("keep the vision secret"). This cannot mean that the message is hidden, for our Lord told us to understand the book of Daniel (Matt. 24:15). Rather, it means that Daniel was to protect and preserve this inspired writing. "The time of the end" refers to eschatological times including the Great Tribulation (cf. 11:35, 40).

Many will go back and forth, and knowledge will increase. The prophet Amos foresaw the days when men "will go to and fro to seek the word of the Lord" (Amos 8:12). Leon Wood points to other passages (e.g., 2 Chron. 16:9; Jer. 5:1; 49:3; Zech. 4:10) where the same form of the verb *šûṭ* used here by Daniel means basically "to move quickly, run to and fro," suggesting "that people would run about trying to find answers to important questions, especially in reference to future events."[33]

"The knowledge" (definite article) which will be increased, in this context, would seem to be that which the preserved book of Daniel supplies to diligent seekers, not only "at the end of time," but at any time subsequent to the preserving (canonically) of the book (cf. Matt. 24:15). "This explanation would give the following paraphrase of the thought: 'Many shall run to and fro in their desire for knowledge of the last things, and, finding it in Daniel's book, because it will have been preserved to this end, their knowledge shall be increased.' "[34]

33. Ibid., p. 321.
34. Ibid., p. 321. Leon Wood's exegetical insights for Daniel 12:4-13 have been particularly helpful to me.

b. An Angel's Question (12:5-7)

12:5-6. Then I, Daniel, looked and behold, two others were standing, one on this bank of the river, and the other on that bank of the river. And one said to the man dressed in linen, who was above the waters of the river, "How long will it be until the end of these wonders?" This took place at the Tigris River (cf. 10:4) and was quite similar to the vision described in 8:13-16. Probably the two angels by this river had been talking together previously, expressing their great interest in human affairs (see 1 Pet. 1:12). The grand angel dressed in linen is the same as that of 10:5. The fact that he was seen *above* the river suggests his supernatural authority and power. "The end of the wonders," in context, must refer to the great seventieth week of Daniel.

12:7. And I heard the man dressed in linen, who was above the waters of the river, as he raised his right hand and his left toward heaven, and swore by Him who lives forever that it would be for a time, times, and half a time; and as soon as they finish shattering the power of the holy people, all these events will be completed. The two hands raised to heaven emphasize the tremendous solemnity of the oath being uttered (cf. Gen. 14:22; Deut. 32:40). The One "who lives forever" is an appropriate name for God (cf. 1 Tim. 6:16; Deut. 32:40). Note the similarity of this event to the one described by John: "and the angel whom I saw standing on the sea and on the land lifted up his right hand to heaven, and swore by Him who lives forever and ever" (Rev. 10:5-6).

The answer that came from this exalted angel was twofold. First, the duration "of these wonders" would be "time, times, and half a time," exactly as Daniel had been told seventeen years earlier (cf. 7:25), namely, three-and-a-half years (i.e., the last half of the seventieth week). Second, the final outcome of this time period would be the complete shattering of the power (Heb., "hand") of "the holy people," that is, regenerate Israel during the Great Tribulation.

Nearly a thousand years earlier, Moses had foreseen these events (cf. Lev. 26; Deut. 28, 30). Isaiah also spoke of this ultimate crisis for the nation (cf. 4:3-4; 6:11-13; 9:4-5; 14:3; 24:1-23; 26:20-21), and so did Jeremiah (30:4-11) and Zechariah (11:15-17; 13:7-9; 14:1-2). The Olivet Discourse of our Lord (Matt. 24-25; Luke 21) picks up and follows through with the same theme, which climaxes in His revelation to John (Rev. 7; 11-12). The Beast and the False Prophet will be God's visible agents (through Satan) to accomplish this "strange work" of crushing the pride and self-sufficiency of Israel, so that she, as a last resort, will cry out, "Blessed is He who comes in the name of the Lord" (Matt. 23:39), and will enter into her millennial rest, having "received of the Lord's hand double for all her sins" (Isa. 40:2).

c. Daniel's Questions (12:8-13)

12:8. As for me, I heard but could not understand; so I said, "My lord, what will be the outcome [Heb., "final end] *of these events?"* "As for me" may suggest that although Daniel did not understand, the angels did. The expression "my lord" does not always refer to deity in Scripture but is used very frequently simply as a term of respect to a superior creature (human or angelic).

Daniel does not ask the question, "How long?" as the angel did (12:6), but rather, "What will finally happen to my people?" If Israel is to be delivered from "the little horn" (7:26-27) and the ultimate "time of distress" (12:1), how will this take place?

12:9. And he said, "Go your way, Daniel, for these words are concealed and sealed up until the end time." "Go your way," not physically, but in the sense of ending the conversation. These God-given words would not evaporate with time and circumstances but would be preserved for the people who will experience their ultimate fulfillment (cf. 12:4). "The end time" generation will possess, and will be comforted by, these very words in the book of Daniel. Daniel's questions were not ignored by God but were answered more fully six hundred years later to John on the isle of Patmos. God's people must learn to

be content with mastering and obeying truth God has already
revealed (cf. Deut. 4:2; 12:32; Prov. 30:5-6; Rev. 22:18-19).

12:10. Many will be purged, purified and refined, but the wicked will act wickedly, and none of the wicked will understand, but those who have insight will understand. The same three
words, "purge," "purify," and "refine," were employed in
11:35 to describe God's chastening work in Israel through the
centuries that followed Antiochus Epiphanes. It should have
been encouraging to Daniel to learn that "many" Israelites
would be thus purified and would "have insight" (cf. 11:35;
12:3). Even during the Great Tribulation there will be 144,000
Israelites sealed by God for global witness (Rev. 7), as well as
thousands of others who will be hidden in "the wilderness" in
"her place . . . from the presence of the serpent" (Rev. 12:14).

It is always important for God's people to realize why it is
that "none of the wicked will understand" prophetic writings
such as the book of Daniel. It is not a lack of academic brilliance, for in contrast to "the wicked," there are actually "not
many wise according to the flesh" among God's people (1 Cor.
1:26). The problem is always spiritual blindness (John 9:39-41;
2 Cor. 3:14-16). "A natural man does not accept the things of
the Spirit of God; for they are foolishness to him, and he cannot understand them, because they are spiritually appraised"
(1 Cor. 2:14). God does not hereby place a premium on ig-
norance (Eph. 5:17), but rather emphasizes the total inac-
cessibity of spiritual wisdom to those who are brilliant but
unregenerate. Such people are "always learning and never able
to come to the knowledge of the truth" (2 Tim. 3:7). Daniel
himself was among those who had spiritual "insight" in his
day, but he did not understand all prophetic truth. However, in
"the end time" Israel will understand Daniel's prophecies as
no previous generation will have been able to understand them.
In the light of this great fact, Daniel could now "go" and be
comforted.

12:11. And from the time that the regular sacrifice is abolished, and the abomination of desolation is set up, there will be 1,290 days. The number of days given in Daniel and Revelation for the duration of the Great Tribulation is 1,260 days. Any extension beyond that, our Lord stated (Matt. 24:22), would result in the total destruction of the human race. What, then, is the significance of the additional 30 days?

The answer lies within the verse itself. The additional thirty days are somehow connected with Antichrist's setting up of "the abomination of desolation" and termination of "the regular sacrifice" in the Temple of God in Jerusalem in the middle of the seventieth week. When our Lord returns to the earth exactly 1,260 days after that event, He will presumably initiate a 30-day cleansing and purification of the Temple of God (cf. 2 Thess. 2:4). Similarly, King Hezekiah postponed by one month the celebration of Passover "because the priests had not consecrated themselves in sufficient numbers, nor had the people been gathered to Jerusalem. Thus the thing was right in the sight of the king and all the assembly" (2 Chron. 30:2-4). Likewise, Judas Maccabaeus and his army went to great lengths to cleanse the Jerusalem Temple of the abominations of Antiochus Epiphanes in 164 B.C. (1 Macc. 4:36-51).

12:12. How blessed is he who keeps waiting and attains to the 1,335 days! The waiting period for survivors of the Great Tribulation is now extended another forty-five days beyond the cleansing of the Temple. Surely this period (and perhaps even the full seventy-five days following the return of Christ) is necessary for the judgment of the living nations to determine publicly who is qualified to enter Messiah's kingdom.

Prophetic Scripture has much to say about this confrontation. Joel placed this future judgment in "the valley of Jehoshaphat [Kidron]," where Gentile mistreatment of Jews will finally be dealt with (Joel 3:1-17). In the same Kidron Valley, Ezra supervised a purging of mixed marriages, a process that required several weeks of careful investigation (Ezra 10:9-17). Ezekiel foretold the ultimate purging of all "rebels" out of Israel before millennial blessing could begin in the Promised Land (Ezek. 20:33-38; also Isa. 4:3-4; Mal. 3:1-6).

The clearest New Testament passage describing this event is

Matthew 25:31-46. Here Christ tells us that Gentiles will be judged in that day according to their treatment of Israelite witnesses ("these brothers of Mine," Matt. 25:40). The fate of those who reject God's messengers, and thus God Himself, is stated in terms of death and eternal judgment (Matt. 25:46); but believers among the Gentiles will be told: "Come, you who are blessed of my Father, inherit the kingdom" (25:34). That, too, is the emphasis in God's answer to Daniel: "How blessed is he . . . !"

Thus, exactly 1,335 days after Antichrist's masterpiece (through the False Prophet) is unveiled in the Temple, Christ's millennial Kingdom begins. "All Israel will be saved" (Rom. 11:26; also Matt. 24:13), for all unbelievers will have been purged out of the nation; and all Gentile believers will be as sheep under one Shepherd (cf. John 10:16), spiritually "blessed" of God the Father.

12:13. But as for you, go your way to the end; then you will enter into rest and rise again for your allotted portion at the end of the age. Daniel himself, with the hope of bodily resurrection ("shall awake," 12:2) and of subsequent service for his God ("those who have insight will shine brightly . . . like the stars forever and ever," 12:3; "blessed is he who . . . attains," (12:12), is now assured that he has sufficient revelation to live and die peacefully (cf. 12:4, 9).

After the "rest" of an intermediate state (between death and resurrection; see 1 Sam. 28:15), which will continue for righteous Jews until "the end of the age" (i.e., the end of the Great Tribulation), Daniel will "rise again" and will enjoy his "lot" (i.e., inheritance; cf. Col. 1:12) during the Kingdom age. He will share this infinite privilege with all "first resurrection" people who "will be priests of God and of Christ and will reign with Him for a thousand years" (Rev. 20:6) over the present earth and then forever in the new heavens and the new earth that God will create for His people (Rev. 21-22).

Like the apostle Paul, faithful Daniel could surely have said: "I know whom I have believed and I am convinced that He is able to guard what I have entrusted to Him until that day"

(2 Tim. 1:12). May that also be our confident expectation as we meditate on the marvelous words our God entrusted to Daniel many years ago.

SELECTED BIBLIOGRAPHY

Archer, Gleason L. "The Aramaic of the 'Genesis Apocryphon' Compared with the Aramaic of Daniel." In *New Perspectives on the Old Testament,* edited by J. Barton Payne, pp. 160-69. Waco, Tex.: Word, 1970.

_____. "Daniel" in vol. 7 of *The Expositor's Bible Commentary.* Grand Rapids: Zondervan, 1985.

_____, trans. *Jerome's Commentary on Daniel.* Grand Rapids: Baker, 1958.

_____. *A Survey of Old Testament Introduction.* Rev. ed. Chicago: Moody, 1974.

Baldwin, Joyce G. *Daniel: An Introduction and Commentary. Tyndale OT Commentaries.* Downers Grove, Ill.: InterVarsity, 1978.

Boutflower Charles. *In and Around the Book of Daniel.* London: SPCK, 1923.

Boyer, James L. *Chart of the Period Between the Testaments.* Winona Lake, Ind.: BMH Books, 1962.

Culver, Robert D. *Daniel and the Latter Days.* Rev. ed. Chicago: Moody, 1977.

Dressler, Harold H. P. "The Identification of the Ugaritic DNIL with the Daniel of Ezekiel." *Vetus Testamentum* 29 (1979):152-61.

Dougherty, Raymond P. *Nabonidus and Belshazzar.* New Haven, Conn.: Yale U., 1929.

Foster, William F. "The Eschatological Significance of the Assyrian in the Old Testament." Th.D. dissertation. Grace Theological Seminary, Winona Lake, Ind., 1956.

France, R. T. *Jesus and the Old Testament.* Grand Rapids: Baker, 1971.

Harrison, R. K. *Introduction to the Old Testament.* Grand Rapids: Eerdmans, 1969.

Harton, George H. "An Interpretation of Daniel 11:36-45." *Grace Theological Journal* 4, no. 2 (Fall 1983):205-31.

Hoehner, Harold W. *Chronological Aspects of the Life of Christ.* Grand Rapids: Zondervan, 1977.

Josephus, Flavius. *Antiquities of the Jews* and *Against Apion.* In *The Works of Flavius Josephus,* translated by William Whiston. 4 vols. Grand Rapids: Eerdmans, 1974.

Keil, C. F. *Biblical Commentary on the Book of Daniel.* Edinburgh: T. & T. Clark, 1872. Reprint. Grand Rapids: Eerdmans, 1955.

Lang, G. H. *The Histories and Prophecies of Daniel.* London: Oliphants, 1942.

Leupold, H. C. *Exposition of Daniel.* Columbus: Wartburg, 1949.

McClain, Alva J. *Daniel's Prophecy of the Seventy Weeks.* Grand Rapids: Zondervan, 1969.

_____. *The Greatness of the Kingdom.* Winona Lake, Ind.: BMH Books, 1959.

McDowell, Josh. *Daniel in the Critics' Den.* San Bernadino, Calif.: Campus Crusade for Christ, 1979.

Millard, A. R. "Daniel 1-6 and History." *The Evangelical Quarterly* 49, no. 2 (April-June 1977):67-73.

Parker, Richard A., and Dubberstein, Waldo H. *Babylonian Chronology 626 B.C.-A.D. 75.* Providence, R.I.: Brown U., 1956.

Parrot, Andre. *Nineveh and Babylon.* New York: Western, Golden, 1961.

Price, Walter K. *In the Final Days.* Chicago: Moody, 1977.

Pritchard, James B., ed. *Ancient Near Eastern Texts Relating to the Old Testament.* 3d ed. with supplement. Princeton: Princeton U., 1969.

Rowe, Robert D. "Is Daniel's 'Son of Man' Messianic?" In *Christ the Lord,* edited by Harold H. Rowden, pp. 71-79. Downer's Grove, Ill.: InterVarsity, 1982.

Tan, Paul Lee. *The Interpretation of Prophecy.* Winona Lake, Ind.: BMH Books, 1974.

Thiele, Edwin R. *The Mysterious Numbers of the Hebrew Kings.* Rev. ed. Grand Rapids: Zondervan, 1983.

Wallace, Daniel B. "A Note On Daniel 1:6—The Relation of Daniel's Daniel to Ezekiel's Daniel." Mimeographed. Winona Lake, Ind.: Grace Theological Seminary, 1982.

Wallace, Ronald S. *The Lord Is King: The Message of Daniel.* Downers Grove, Ill.: InterVarsity, 1979.

Walvoord, John F. *Daniel: The Key to Prophetic Revelation.* Chicago: Moody, 1971.

Whitcomb, John C. *Chart of the Babylonian Captivity.* Winona Lake, Ind.: Grace Theological Seminary, 1962.

_____. *Chart of Old Testament Kings and Prophets.* 5th ed. rev. Winona Lake, Ind.: Grace Theological Seminary, 1977.

_____. "Cyrus in the Prophecies of Isaiah." In *The Law and the Prophets,* edited by John H. Skilton, pp. 388-401. Phillipsburg, N.J.: Presbyterian & Reformed, 1974.

_____. "Daniel." In *The Illustrated Bible Dictionary,* 3 vols. Wheaton: Tyndale, 1980.

_____. "Daniel's Great Seventy-Week Prophecy: An Exegetical Insight." *Grace Theological Journal* 2, no. 2 (Fall 1981): 259-63.

_____. *Darius the Mede: The Historical Chronology of Daniel.* Phillipsburg, N.J.: Presbyterian & Reformed, 1959.

_____. *Esther: Triumph of God's Sovereignty.* Chicago: Moody, 1979.

_____. *Solomon to the Exile: Studies in Kings and Chronicles.* Grand Rapids: Baker, 1971.

Wilson, Robert Dick. *Studies in the Book of Daniel.* New York: Knickerbocker, 1917.

Wiseman, Donald J. *Chronicles of Chaldean Kings (626-556 B.C.).* London: Trustees of the British Museum, 1961.

_____ et al., eds. *Notes on Some Problems in the Book of Daniel.* London: Tyndale, 1965.

Wood, Leon J. *A Commentary on Daniel.* Grand Rapids: Zondervan, 1973.

Yamauchi, Edwin Y. "The Archaeological Background of Daniel." *Bibliotheca Sacra* 137, no. 545 (January-March 1981):37-47.

Young, Edward J. *The Prophecy of Daniel.* Grand Rapids: Eerdmans, 1949.

DANIEL AND HIS CONTEMPORARIES

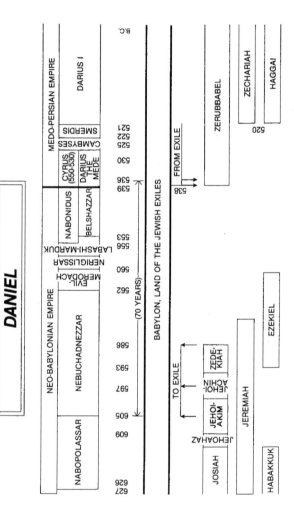

DANIEL

TIMES OF DANIEL

c.615 B.C.—Habakkuk foresees rise of Babylon

612 B.C.—Fall of Nineveh

609 B.C.—Josiah killed at Megiddo by Necho II of Egypt

605 B.C.—Jeremiah prophesies 70-year captivity

—Daniel and three friends taken to Babylon

602 B.C.—Daniel interprets dream of great image

(Dan.2)

597 B.C.—Jehoiachin deported by Nebuchadnezzar

593 B.C.—Daniel's wisdom well-known;

Ezekiel's first vision

586 B.C.—Jerusalem falls; Jeremiah and others go to Egypt

573 B.C.—Ezekiel's vision of Millennial Temple

553 B.C.—Daniel's vision of four beasts

551 B.C.—Daniel's vision of ram and male goat

---

70 Years Captivity, 605-536 B.C.

---

539 B.C.—Daniel's vision of 70 weeks;

Cyrus the Great conquers Babylon

538 B.C.—Jews encouraged to return to Palestine

537 B.C.—Jews set up altar in Jerusalem

536 B.C.—Daniel's final great vision;

foundation of second Temple laid

520 B.C.—Work on Temple resumed

516 B.C.—Second Temple finished

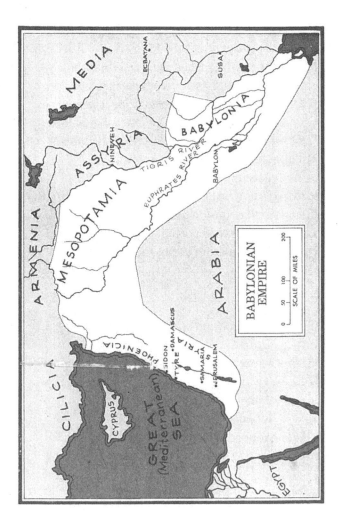

BABYLONIAN EMPIRE

SCALE OF MILES
0   50   100   200

MEDIA

ECBATANA

SUSA

BABYLONIA

ASSYRIA

NINEVEH

BABYLON

TIGRIS RIVER

EUPHRATES RIVER

ARMENIA

MESOPOTAMIA

ARABIA

CILICIA

PHOENICIA

SIDON

TYRE

DAMASCUS

SYRIA

SAMARIA

JERUSALEM

CYPRUS

GREAT
(Mediterranean)
SEA

EGYPT